THE ULTIMATE
CHICAGO BLACKHAWKS
TRIVIA BOOK

A Collection of Amazing Trivia Quizzes
and Fun Facts for Die-Hard Blackhawks Fans!

Ray Walker

ISBN: 978-1-953563-19-4

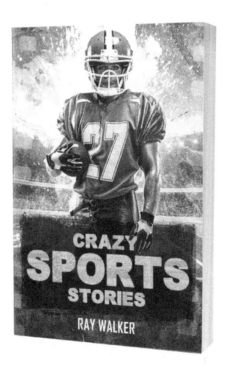

CONTENTS

INTRODUCTION

When it comes to hockey fans, the legendary Chicago Blackhawks supporters are known across the globe as being among the most passionate and vocal. This historic NHL franchise has been attracting new fans, year after year, since joining the league in 1926-27. Those who follow the Windy City's club certainly know their hockey and have had the pleasure of seeing their squad hoist the Stanley Cup on half a dozen occasions as of 2019.

Blackhawks fans know their club isn't perfect and have had to endure several low points to accompany the highs. They're not afraid to speak their mind and let the players know, in no uncertain terms, if they're not pulling their weight. But the fans are also fiercely proud when pulling on the famous Chicago jersey and rooting for their team.

Being one of the NHL's "Original Six" franchises, the Blackhawks have simply oozed hockey history from their famous arenas, such as the Chicago Coliseum, Chicago Stadium, and United Center. The fans have had the great fortune of seeing some of the world's best players skate at these rinks, including Hockey Hall-of-Famers Bobby Hull, Stan Mikita, and Tony Esposito.

This compact Chicago Blackhawks trivia and fact book helps celebrate the team's history from day one to the completion of the 2019-20 regular season. It's going to be a wonderful, yet educational trip.

The book provides 15 different chapters, each with an interesting topic on the Hawks' colorful history. It's the perfect way to challenge yourself and others when it comes to knowledge of your favorite hockey team. You'll find that each section features a mixture of 20 multiple choice and true-false questions, with answers on a separate page, and 10 "Did You Know" facts about the franchise.

This trivia book aims to educate and entertain fans about the Chicago Blackhawks and is the ideal tool to use when taking on fellow Hawks fans in trivia challenges. Whatever your reason is for reading the book, it's sure to strengthen your bond with the Blackhawks.

The facts, statistics, and information featured here are up to date as of the beginning of 2020. While the Hawks haven't been flying that high lately, they're bound to soar again soon.

This book will reignite your love for the team and help solidify your position as an authority on the Blackhawks.

CHAPTER 1:

ORIGINS & HISTORY

QUIZ TIME!

1. Who did Chicago play their first NHL game against?

   a. Boston Bruins

   b. Detroit Cougars

   c. Toronto St. Patricks

   d. New York Americans

2. Which team did the Blackhawks defeat to win their first Stanley Cup?

   a. New York Rangers

   b. Detroit Red Wings

   c. Boston Bruins

   d. Montreal Maroons

3. Chicago was the first NHL team to have a roster made up of only American-born players.

   a. True

   b. False

4. How many appearances has the franchise made in the Stanley Cup Final?

    a. 16
    b. 10
    c. 13
    d. 15

5. What was the final score in the team's first victory?

    a. 1-0
    b. 4-3
    c. 2-0
    d. 4-1

6. The Blackhawks have had how many coaches as of 2020?

    a. 40
    b. 38
    c. 29
    d. 35

7. Who was the very first owner of the franchise?

    a. Huntington Hardwick
    b. Charles Adams
    c. James E. Norris
    d. Frederic McLaughlin

8. The squad finished its inaugural season with a record of 24-17-4.

    a. True
    b. False

9. When did the Blackhawks make their first playoff appearance?

    a. 1926-27

    b. 1929-30

    c. 1933-34

    d. 1932-33

10. As of 2019, the club has won how many Stanley Cups?

    a. 5

    b. 4

    c. 7

    d. 6

11. The team had a total of seven different coaches in their first four seasons.

    a. True

    b. False

12. In which season did the Hawks finish with 52 wins?

    a. 2013-14

    b. 2010-11

    c. 2009-10

    d. 2008-09

13. Chicago completed their first season with how many points?

    a. 54

    b. 44

    c. 36

    d. 41

14. Between 1944 and 1958, the team made the playoffs just twice.

    a. True
    b. False

15. How many games did the Blackhawks win from 1927-28 to 1928-29?

    a. 47
    b. 55
    c. 14
    d. 12

16. How many franchise members have been inducted into the Hockey Hall of Fame as players?

    a. 39
    b. 26
    c. 40
    d. 44

17. Where did Chicago play their home games in their first NHL campaign?

    a. United Center
    b. Chicago Coliseum
    c. Chicago Stadium
    d. Peace Bridge Arena

18. What season were the Blackhawks placed in the NHL's Central Division?

    a. 1993-94
    b. 1994-95

c. 1995-96

d. 1996-97

19. Who was the first coach of the club?

    a. Dick Irvin

    b. Hugh Lehman

    c. Pete Muldoon

    d. Barney Stanley

20. James E. Norris was involved with just one other NHL team while serving as owner of the Blackhawks.

    a. True

    b. False

QUIZ ANSWERS

1. C – Toronto St. Patricks

2. B – Detroit Red Wings

3. A – True

4. C – 13

5. D – 4-1

6. B – 38

7. A – Huntington Hardwick

8. B – False

9. A – 1926-27

10. D – 6

11. A – True

12. C – 2009-10

13. D – 41

14. A – True

15. C – 14

16. D – 44

17. B – Chicago Coliseum

18. A – 1993-94

19. C – Pete Muldoon

20. B – False

DID YOU KNOW?

1. The Chicago Blackhawks are based in Chicago, Illinois, and were founded in 1926. They made their NHL debut in 1926-27 season and were known as the Black Hawks up until 1986. The franchise then changed the spelling to Blackhawks. The club currently competes in the Western Conference in the Central Division.

2. Chicago is known as one of the NHL's Original Six teams and has won the Stanley Cup six times. The team's first home rink was the Chicago Coliseum, and they moved to the Chicago Stadium in 1929. They played at the Stadium for 65 years before moving to the United Center in 1994. They share the current venue with the Chicago Bulls of the National Basketball Association (NBA).

3. The first owner of the franchise was coffee tycoon Frederic McLaughlin, until he died in 1944. The Norris family and partner Bill Tobin then took over. Norris also owned the Chicago Stadium as well as majority ownership stakes in the New York Rangers and Detroit Red Wings. When James E. Norris died in 1952, his son James D. Norris took over as owner of the franchise.

4. James D. Norris died in 1966, and the club fell under the ownership of the Wirtz family, headed by Arthur Wirtz with support from his son Bill. When Arthur died in 1983, Bill took over; and when he died in 2007, his son Rocky

Wirtz assumed control of the Wirtz Corporation. He helped turned the team's fortunes around with a trio of Stanley Cup wins from 2010 to 2015.

5. The Chicago franchise was originally awarded on May 1, 1926, to a syndicate headed by Huntington Hardwick, a former football player. Hardwick then paid $100,000 for the players from the Portland Rosebuds club of the Western Hockey League (WHL) to help fill Chicago's roster. But just a month later, Hardwick's syndicate sold the franchise to Frederic McLaughlin.

6. Frederic McLaughlin was commander of a military unit nicknamed "The Blackhawk Division" during World War II. The Blackhawk name was in honor of the Sauk nation of Native American Indians and were a large part of history in the state of Illinois. McLaughlin then named his franchise in honor of the military division and Sauk nation.

7. The city of Chicago had two hockey clubs in 1926-27 as the Chicago Cardinals of the American Hockey Association (AHA) also played out of the Chicago Coliseum. The Cardinals lasted just one season at the location though.

8. The Blackhawks were scheduled to play the 1928-29 campaign at the Chicago Stadium, but the building's opening was plagued by construction delays. This meant the season's home games were divided between the Chicago Coliseum, the Peace Bridge Arena in Fort Erie, Canada, and the Detroit Olympia. The club moved into the

Chicago Stadium in time for the 1929-30 season. The Stadium's ice surface was smaller than the regular 200 feet by 85 feet size of an NHL rink, as it measured 185 feet by 85 feet.

9. Chicago first hoisted the Stanley Cup in 1933-34, with the most recent being 2014-15. The team was considered an NHL dynasty a decade ago, winning championships in 2009-10, 2012-13, and 2014-15. They also won the President's Trophy as the NHL's top team in the regular season in 2012-13.

10. The Blackhawks have two Minor League affiliate franchises. These are the Rockford Ice Hogs of the American Hockey League (AHL) and the Indy Fuel of the East Coast Hockey League (ECHL). Chicago's television broadcaster is NBC Sports Chicago, while their radio broadcasts are handled by WGN Radio.

CHAPTER 2:

JERSEYS & NUMBERS

QUIZ TIME!

1. How many numbers have been retired by the franchise?

    a. 4

    b. 5

    c. 6

    d. 7

2. What year did the Blackhawks begin to wear a second jersey?

    a. 1940

    b. 1939

    c. 1929

    d. 1931

3. What number did emergency backup goalie Scott Foster wear in 2018?

    a. 44

    b. 37

    c. 89

    d. 90

4. Which number has been worn by 47 different players?

    a. 14

    b. 6

    c. 17

    d. 8

5. When did the Blackhawks introduce a touch of red to their black and white jersey?

    a. 1957

    b. 1954

    c. 1956

    d. 1934

6. Stan Mikita was the first player to have his number retired by the franchise.

    a. True

    b. False

7. Which retired number was worn by both Keith Magnuson and Pierre Pilote?

    a. 15

    b. 4

    c. 3

    d. 18

8. Patrick Kane originally wore number 15.

    a. True

    b. False

9. What number did Marian Hossa wear from 2010 to 2017?

a. 93

b. 68

c. 81

d. 80

10. When was Bobby Hull's number retired?

a. 1988

b. 1985

c. 1982

d. 1983

11. Tony Esposito is the only player to wear number 35 with the club.

a. True

b. False

12. Which player had their number 18 retired?

a. Darcy Rota

b. Jim McFadden

c. Gerry Pinder

d. Denis Savard

13. What number did Phil Esposito wear in Chicago?

a. 11

b. 5

c. 7

d. 8

14. The Blackhawks have only used two different designs for regular-season alternate jerseys.

a. True

b. False

15. Which number did Bobby Hull NOT wear while in Chicago?

    a. 9

    b. 14

    c. 16

    d. 7

16. Who started to wear the number 65 in 2012?

    a. Gustav Forsling

    b. Brandon Bollig

    c. Trevor Van Riemsdyk

    d. Andrew Shaw

17. When did the franchise start wearing an alternate jersey?

    a. 1996

    b. 1997

    c. 1999

    d. 1995

18. Which number has NOT been worn by a Chicago player?

    a. 74

    b. 31

    c. 64

    d. 61

19. Who became the second player to wear the number 58 in 2006-07?

a. Jeff Hamilton
b. Karl Stewart
c. P.A. Parenteau
d. Ivan Droppa

20. The number 51 is the most popular number worn by more than 50 players on the team.

a. True
b. False

QUIZ ANSWERS

1. C – 6

2. A – 1940

3. D – 90

4. B – 6

5. D – 1934

6. A – True

7. C – 3

8. B – False

9. C – 81

10. D – 1983

11. A – True

12. D – Denis Savard

13. C – 7

14. A – True

15. B – 14

16. D – Andrew Shaw

17. A – 1996

18. D – 61

19. C – P.A. Parenteau

20. B – False

DID YOU KNOW?

1. Chicago jerseys are predominantly dark red with black-and-white striped trimming or predominantly white with dark red and black trimming. The club has also used alternate black jerseys with red-and-white or black-and-white stripes. The franchise logo is the head of a Native American Indian with feathers in his hair facing downward. When the club joined the league, the predominant colors were black and white.

2. Irene Castle, the wife of early team owner Frederic McLaughlin, was the designer of the original logo. This featured a black and white Native American head inside of a circle. The logo was altered several times until 1955, with seven different logos being used. The biggest change came in 1955 when the circle was removed and just the Native American head was left.

3. In 2004, *Gentleman's Quarterly Magazine* named the uniform as one of the top 25 in all of professional sports. The *Hockey News* publication has also voted the club's jersey as the NHL's best, and a fan vote in 2017 named the uniform as the best in NHL history.

4. Six different jersey numbers have been retired by the Blackhawks. The number 1 was retired in honor of goaltender Glenn Hall while 3 is to honor defenders Keith Magnuson and Pierre Pilote. The number 9 used to belong

to winger Bobby Hull, while 18 was worn by center Denis Savard. Number 21 belonged to center Stan Mikita, and 35 was worn by goaltender Tony Esposito.

5. The most popular jersey number in team annals has been the number 6, with 47 different players wearing it. The number 14 has also been quite popular, with 41 players choosing to wear it. Players who have worn number 6 include Phil Housley and Bob Murray, while Ken Hodge, Wayne Maki, and Al Secord are among those who donned number 14.

6. The lowest jersey number worn by Blackhawks players has been number 1, which was worn by 18 of the team's goaltenders. The highest number worn by a Chicago player has been 95, which Dylan Sikura started wearing in 2018.

7. Every jersey number between 1 and 60 has been worn by at least one Blackhawks player. In addition, 23 numbers between 62 and 95 have been worn at least once. The famous number 9 was worn by seven other players before Bobby Hull took it over from 1964 to 1972. Hull wore 16 and 7 before switching to 9.

8. Number 13 has long been considered an unlucky number by many, and this seems to be the case with Blackhawks players. Nobody wore the number until Alexei Zhamnov tested the superstition in the year 2000. Since then, Daniel Carcillo and Tomas Jurco have also given it a go.

9. A total of 22 players have worn number 2 for Chicago, with two of them being inducted into the Hockey Hall of

Fame. Jack Stewart wore it from 1951 to 1952, and fellow defenseman Al Arbour donned it from 1959 to 1961. Stewart was inducted into the Hall as a player, while Arbour was enshrined as a builder.

10. Some fans may have forgotten that the great Bobby Orr played with Chicago from 1976-77 to 1978-79. The blueliner wore the number 4 he made famous in Boston. However, his number wasn't retired by the Blackhawks as he played just 26 regular-season games with the club due to injuries. Nine Blackhawks have worn number 4 since Orr retired.

CHAPTER 3:

FAMOUS QUOTES

QUIZ TIME!

1. When speaking about former coach Mike Keenan, which Chicago player stated, "The veterans on the team didn't fear Keenan; they merely despised him, and I believe Mike liked it that way."?
   a. Bob Bassen
   b. Mike Eagles
   c. Jeremy Roenick
   d. Ed Belfour

2. Which teammate was Johnny Oduya speaking about when he said, "He's a tough character, he's a Swedish Viking."?
   a. Niklas Hjalmarsson
   b. Joakim Nordstrom
   c. Marcus Kruger
   d. Tim Erixon

3. When asked how he could play with a fractured ankle, former blueliner Boris Mironov replied, "I just tape four Tylenols to it."

e. True

f. False

4. Which Blackhawk stated, "My teeth weren't that good to begin with. Hopefully I can get some better ones."?

    a. Duncan Keith

    b. Dominik Kubalik

    c. Alex DeBrincat

    d. Alexander Nylander

5. "Once you win the Stanley Cup you feel like it's yours and don't want to give it up," was said by which Hawk?

    a. Coach Joel Quenneville

    b. Jonathan Toews

    c. Corey Crawford

    d. Patrick Sharp

6. This quote was said by which former Blackhawk: "Yeah, I'm cocky and arrogant. But that doesn't mean I'm not a nice person."?

    a. Coach Mike Keenan

    b. Dave Manson

    c. Jeremy Roenick

    d. Bryan Marchment

7. A former Hawk once said, "I was a multi-millionaire from playing hockey. Then I got divorced, and now I am a millionaire." Who was it?

    a. Stan Mikita

    b. Phil Esposito

c. Bobby Hull

d. Denis Savard

8. After losing a playoff game, winger Brandon Saad once claimed, "I slept like a baby. Every two hours, I woke up and cried."

    a. True

    b. False

9. After taking a puck to the face and sporting bruises, this Hawk told the media, "I don't know if it's a badge of honor, but it looks pretty cool."

    c. Murray Bannerman

    d. Andrew Shaw

    e. Dylan Strome

    f. Zack Smith

10. When asked if he would be back from injury for the playoffs, this Hawk stated, "I don't know about percentage, but I'm halfway there."

    a. Bryan Bickell

    b. Jamal Myers

    c. Dave Bolland

    d. Brandon Bollig

11. Television broadcaster Harry Neale once said this when covering a Blackhawks game: "I went to a restaurant in Chicago and they had a no-shooting section."

    a. True

    b. False

12. When coach Joel Quenneville said after a win against Calgary, "That was criminal. They've got to call the cops after that performance. He stole two points," which goaltender was he referring to?

    a. Craig Anderson
    b. Ray Emery
    c. Scott Darling
    d. Corey Crawford

13. Who was Patrick Sharp referring to in 2013 when he called a teammate "Mr. Overtime"?

    a. Patrick Kane
    b. Jonathan Toews
    c. Duncan Keith
    d. Brent Seabrook

14. Goalie Darren Pang once stated, "I'm just glad it wasn't machete night," after fans threw plastic mugs onto the ice during a mug night promotion.

    a. True
    b. False

15. This quote was attributed to which player: "There are some guys you definitely would not want dating your sister, especially hockey players."?

    a. Carter Hutton
    b. Matthew Barnaby
    c. Patrick Kane
    d. Stu Grimson

16. Who once claimed, "If you play to win as I do the game never ends."?

    a. Marian Hossa
    b. Stan Mikita
    c. Bruce Cassidy
    d. Jim Dowd

17. Which Blackhawks coach remarked, "The opportunity is definitely there. Somebody's got to seize it."?

    a. Darryl Sutter
    b. Brian Sutter
    c. Joel Quenneville
    d. Jeremy Colliton

18. Which Chicago netminder said, "Gary Bettman has only a marginal interest in the weaker teams. He only wants the NHL to make a bigger profit as a whole."?

    a. Patrick Lalime
    b. Dominik Hasek
    c. Antti Niemi
    d. Jeff Hackett

19. After stopping Sergei Fedorov on a breakaway, which Chicago goalie said, "He shot it right in my jock strap, so it was a good break for me."?

    a. Jocelyn Thibault
    b. Adam Munro
    c. Michael Leighton
    d. Cristobal Huet

20. "I don't skate to where the puck is, I skate to where it's going to be." This famous quote came from the Hawks' Doug Gilmour.

    a. True
    b. False

QUIZ ANSWERS

1. C – Jeremy Roenick

2. A – Niklas Hjalmarsson

3. A – True

4. A – Duncan Keith

5. B – Jonathan Toews

6. C – Jeremy Roenick

7. C – Bobby Hull

8. B – False

9. B – Andrew Shaw

10. C – Dave Bolland

11. A – True

12. B – Ray Emery

13. D – Brent Seabrook

14. B – False

15. C – Patrick Kane

16. B – Stan Mikita

17. C – Joel Quenneville

18. B – Dominik Hasek

19. A – Jocelyn Thibault

20. B – False

DID YOU KNOW?

1. Head coach Pete Muldoon was fired after the 1927 playoffs, and *The Globe and Mail* newspaper reported that he told team owner Frederic McLaughlin, "Fire me, and you'll never finish first. I'll put a curse on this team that will hoodoo it until the end of time." This became known as "The Curse of Muldoon." However, reporter Jim Coleman admitted later that he made the incident up.

2. In February 2004, the ESPN television network named the Blackhawks franchise as the worst in professional sports for various reasons. At the time, the Chicago Wolves of the American Hockey League (AHL) poked fun at them by coming up with a marketing campaign with the quote, "We Play Hockey the Old-Fashioned Way: We Actually Win."

3. When a Montreal Canadiens star used to score at the Montreal Forum in the 1950s and '60s, fans would often celebrate by throwing toe rubbers for boots onto the ice. Former Chicago winger Dennis Hull claims his father asked him before a game, "Son, when the Habs score tonight and the rubbers hit the ice, grab me a good pair, will you? Size 10."

4. Head coach Mike Keenan had the reputation of being tough to please, and former Hawk Jeremy Roenick once wrote, "The truth is, Keenan scared me into being a better

NHL player. I was 18 when I began to play for Iron Mike, and I was afraid of him. As a rookie, I felt as if my future depended on pleasing Keenan."

5. American President Barack Obama stated this after the Hawks won the Stanley Cup in 2013: "To the Bulls, Bears, Cubs, White Sox, I am term limited, so you guys got to get moving. I need to see you here soon. Championships belong in Chicago. So, to the Blackhawks, thank you for bringing them back home. Thank you for bringing the Stanley Cup."

6. Legendary Hall-of-Famer Stan Mikita once said, "There are rough players and there are dirty players. I'm rough and dirty." The classy center won two Lady Byng Trophies for gentlemanly conduct and sportsmanship but also served 1,270 minutes in penalties. However, he served just a combined 26 minutes in the seasons he won the award.

7. Goaltending great Dominik Hasek was thankful for every point earned but wasn't the biggest fan of shootouts. He once said, "It's definitely a great feeling to win the game and to win in the shootout. You get the extra one point which is great, but I would rather win the game in 60 minutes or in the regular overtime."

8. Patrick Kane was drafted 1st overall in 2007 and played his first NHL game just four months later. The high-scoring forward remarked, "For me, I was really lucky to go to a city like Chicago where the team was struggling at the time, and I was able to go in and play right away."

9. The famous "Golden Jet" Bobby Hull had this to say about his son 'The Golden Brett': "Somewhere in my wildest childhood I must have done something right. Being able to make a boyhood dream come true is one thing, but to have a kid come along and thrill his dad like Brett Hull has thrilled me over his career is too much for one guy to handle."

10. After Ted Lindsay tried to unionize the Detroit Red Wings, he was promptly traded to Chicago in 1957. When arriving in the Windy City after playing 13 seasons with Detroit, the Future Hall of Fame winger told the press, "My penalty for rocking the boat was being traded." Lindsay returned to the Red Wings for one final season in 1964-65.

CHAPTER 4:

CATCHY NICKNAMES

QUIZ TIME!

1. What was the nickname of Chicago's English-born winger Steve Thomas?

    a. Stocky
    b. Stumpy
    c. Fish and Chips
    d. The London Fog

2. Which Blackhawks winger was known as "Squid"?

    a. Al Secord
    b. Rick Vaive
    c. Rene Bourque
    d. Bob Bailey

3. "Dominator" was the moniker given to this Chicago goalie.

    a. Dominik Hasek
    b. Corey Crawford
    c. Cam Ward
    d. Gary Smith

4. This defender was known as "Big Daddy."

   a. Bob McGill

   b. Bobby Orr

   c. Adrian Aucoin

   d. Randy Boyd

5. What was goalie Tony Esposito's nickname?

   a. The Godfather

   b. Tony-O

   c. Espo

   d. Eppy

6. Bobby Hull was known as "The Golden Jet."

   a. True

   b. False

7. What was "Buster" Brayshaw's given name?

   a. Russell

   b. Winston

   c. Barry

   d. Robert

8. Who was known as "Babe"?

   a. Cecil Dye

   b. Ben Eager

   c. Bill Gadsby

   d. Bill Gardner

9. Winger Walter Farrant was nicknamed "Whitey." Which defenseman shared the same moniker?

a. Bill White

b. Bryan Marchment

c. Joe Matte

d. Pat Stapleton

10. The nickname "Battleship" was given to which Blackhawk?

a. Wendel Clark

b. Brian Campbell

c. Bob Kelly

d. Billy Burch

11. Clarence John Abel was nicknamed "Taffy."

a. True

b. False

12. "Chico" was the nickname given to which Blackhawk?

a. Patrick Kane

b. Kris King

c. Wayne Maki

d. Ron Maki

13. Bobby Orr never had a nickname but was generally known as "Number Four."

a. True

b. False

14. Winger Hillary "Minnie" Menard played in just one NHL game with Chicago.

a. True

b. False

15. Which of these Chicago defensemen was known as "Red"?

    a. Gary Nylund
    b. Bill Mitchell
    c. Mike O'Connell
    d. Kent Paynter

16. Winger Lawrence Northcott played in 1938-39 and was known as "Baldy."

    a. True
    b. False

17. Which Chicago winger was simply nicknamed "Bud"?

    a. Igor Radulov
    b. Dave Richardson
    c. Gerry Pinder
    d. Norman Poile

18. Which forward was naturally nicknamed "Elvis" by his teammates?

    a. Wayne Presley
    b. Reggie Fleming
    c. Dennis Hull
    d. Patrick Poulin

19. Which Chicago player is known as "Tazer"?

    a. Patrick Kane
    b. Jonathan Toews
    c. Kirby Dach
    d. Andrew Shaw

20. Which Blackhawks rearguard was given the moniker "Bouncer"?

    a. Michal Sykora
    b. Danny Richmond
    c. Craig Muni
    d. Ralph Taylor

QUIZ ANSWERS

1. B – Stumpy

2. B – Rick Vaive

3. A – Dominik Hasek

4. A – Bob McGill

5. B – Tony-O

6. A – True

7. A – Russell

8. A – Cecil Dye

9. D – Pat Stapleton

10. C – Bob Kelly

11. A – True

12. C – Wayne Maki

13. A – True

14. A – True

15. B – Bill Mitchell

16. A – True

17. D – Norman Poile

18. A – Wayne Presley

19. B – Jonathan Toews

20. D – Ralph Taylor

DID YOU KNOW?

1. The city of Chicago, which sits on the shore of Lake Michigan, is nicknamed "The Windy City." The Blackhawks franchise doesn't have a nickname, but many fans simply shorten the name of the team to "The Hawks."

2. Bob "Mad Dog" Kelly earned his nickname with the Philadelphia Flyers, while Bob "Battleship" Kelly played with Chicago, St. Louis, and Pittsburgh in the mid-1970s. At 6 feet 2 inches tall, "Battleship" didn't mind dropping the gloves and served over 100 minutes in penalties in four consecutive seasons. He also posted a pair of 25-plus goal seasons with Pittsburgh.

3. Former Chicago goalie Nikolai Khabibulin was known as "The Bulin Wall," which was based on The Berlin Wall. The Russian-born goalie played with the Hawks from 2005 to 2009 and again in 2013-14. He earned the nickname because he was so hard to score against.

4. Goaltender Gary Smith was known throughout the hockey world as "Suitcase" Smith because he played for so many teams during his NHL career. He played with Chicago from 1971 to 1973 and shared the Vezina Trophy for the least goals against with Tony Esposito in 1971-72.

5. Forward Camille Henry was nicknamed "The Eel" since he was such a slippery player. He was the NHL's rookie of the year in 1953-54 and won the Lady Byng Trophy for his

sportsmanship in 1957-58. Henry played just 22 regular-season contests with Chicago though in 1964-65, as well as 14 playoff games.

6. Al Arbour was known for his excellent coaching career, but before that, he was a solid NHL defenseman. He played 180 regular-season games with Chicago from 1958 to 1961 and was one of the few NHL players to wear eyeglasses on the ice. He earned the nickname "Radar" because of this and because he resembled the Radar O'Reilly character from the TV show and movie *M*A*S*H*.

7. Between 1971 and 1973, the Hawks had a beast on the blue line in the form of Jerry "King Kong" Korab. The 6 foot 3 inch, 220 lb. Korab was one of the biggest players on the ice in that era. He tallied 41 points in 150 regular-season outings with the team and helped Chicago reach the Stanley Cup Final in 1972-73.

8. Defender Dave Manson skated with Chicago from 1986 to 1991 and again from 1988 to 2000. Manson was known for his mean streak and was nicknamed "Charlie" after the infamous cult leader and convicted murderer Charles Manson. He served 2,792 penalty minutes in his 1,103-game career with another 343 minutes in 112 playoff games.

9. Hall of Fame center Howie Morenz played for Chicago in 1934-35 and half of the following season. Before turning pro, he played in the town of Stratford, Canada, and was known as "The Stratford Streak" due to his blinding

speed. The three-time Hart Trophy winner broke his leg in a game in 1937 and died at the age of 34 on March 8 due to complications caused by the injury.

10. The face of the Chicago franchise from 1957 to 1972 was left winger Bobby Hull, who was nicknamed "The Golden Jet" due to his speed and flowing blonde hair. Hull was the first NHLer to score over 50 goals in a season and was known for his ferocious slapshot. He was inducted into the Hockey Hall of Fame in 1983.

CHAPTER 5:

THE CAPTAIN CLASS

QUIZ TIME!

1. How many years has Jonathan Toews been captain, including 2019-20?

    a. 12

    b. 13

    c. 9

    d. 10

2. Who was the first captain in franchise history?

    a. Duke Dukowski

    b. Dick Irvin

    c. Ty Arbour

    d. Helge Bostrom

3. 3. The oldest captain in the club's history was Helge Bostrom at 39 years old.

    a. True

    b. False

4. How many goals did Dirk Graham score in his first year as captain in 1988-89?

   a. 15
   b. 28
   c. 40
   d. 33

5. As of 2019-20, how many captains has Chicago named?

   a. 30
   b. 35
   c. 34
   d. 31

6. Before Jonathan Toews, who was the youngest captain of the Blackhawks?

   a. Terry Ruskowski
   b. Bill Gadsby
   c. Darryl Sutter
   d. Gaye Stewart

7. Captain Johnny Gottselig led the team in points in the 1937-38 playoffs totaling how many?

   a. 9
   b. 8
   c. 10
   d. 6

8. The Blackhawks have never had a goaltender as captain.

   a. True
   b. False

9. Who was Chicago's captain from 1962 to 1968?

   a. Gus Mortson
   b. Pat Stapleton
   c. Ed Litzenberger
   d. Pierre Pilote

10. Who was NOT one of the three players to hold the captaincy in 1976-77?

   a. Stan Mikita
   b. Ivan Boldirev
   c. Pit Martin
   d. Keith Magnuson

11. Terry Ruskowski recorded 597 penalty minutes as the team's captain in three seasons.

   a. True
   b. False

12. How many wins did Charlie Gardiner post as captain of the Blackhawks?

   a. 19
   b. 25
   c. 24
   d. 20

13. Which captain has scored the most goals in a single season as of the end of 2019-20?

   a. Doug Bentley
   b. Jonathan Toews
   c. Dennis Savard
   d. Tony Amonte

14. From 1971 to 1974, the Blackhawks had three different captains.

    a. True
    b. False

15. What was Adrian Aucoin's plus/minus in the 2006-07 season?

    a. -17
    b. -22
    c. +8
    d. +15

16. How many players have served as interim captain for the Blackhawks?

    a. 4
    b. 3
    c. 1
    d. 2

17. Darryl Sutter led the club in goals during the 1984-85 playoffs tallying how many?

    a. 12
    b. 15
    c. 9
    d. 13

18. Which captain sported a plus/minus of -30 in 2005-06?

    a. Tony Amonte
    b. Alexei Zhamnov
    c. Martin Lapointe
    d. Adrian Aucoin

19. How many penalty minutes did Dirk Graham serve in the 1991-92 season?

    a. 106
    b. 92
    c. 63
    d. 89

20. Denis Savard served as captain for just one season.

    a. True
    b. False

QUIZ ANSWERS

1. A – 12

2. B – Dick Irvin

3. A – True

4. D – 33

5. C – 34

6. C – Darryl Sutter

7. B – 8

8. B – False

9. D – Pierre Pilote

10. B – Ivan Boldirev

11. A – True

12. D – 20

13. A – Doug Bentley

14. B – False

15. B – -22

16. D – 2

17. A – 12

18. C – Martin Lapointe

19. D – 89

20. A – True

DID YOU KNOW?

1. The Blackhawks have had 34 different players wear the C on their sweater since the team's inception. Dick Irvin was the first from 1926 to 1929, with Jonathan Toews being the latest since 2008. Pit Martin, Stan Mikita, and Keith Magnuson all wore the C at one point in 1976-77. In addition, Bob Murray was listed as interim captain in 1985-86, with Martin Lapointe as interim in 2006.

2. A total of 13 former Hawks skippers have been inducted into the Hockey Hall of Fame. These are: Dick Irvin, Charlie Gardiner, Earl Seibert, Doug Bentley, Clint Smith, John Mariucci, Jack Stewart, Bill Gadsby, Pierre Pilote, Stan Mikita, Denis Savard, Doug Gilmour, and Chris Chelios. John Mariucci was enshrined in the builders category.

3. The longest-serving Chicago captain is Jonathan Toews, who was appointed for the 2008-09 season and was still holding the position at the conclusion of 2019-20. He's also been the youngest captain in team history as he was just 20 years old when appointed.

4. The oldest player to act as team captain was 39-year-old Helge Bostrom when he was given the honor for 1932-33. In addition, Bostrom also holds the record for the shortest reign as captain at just 20 games. The low-scoring defenseman played four seasons for the club with six points in 96 regular-season games.

5. The Blackhawks named goaltender Charlie Gardiner as captain for 1933-34. The Scottish-born Gardiner made history by becoming the only NHL netminder to skipper his team to a Stanley Cup triumph. The goalie was named to four All-Star Teams and won two Vezina Trophies with Chicago in seven seasons. Sadly, he died at the age of 29 following complications from a tonsil infection in 1934.

6. There has been a mixture of skill and brawn when it comes to captains, as several of them served more than 100 penalty minutes a season. These include Martin Lapointe (106 PIM), Chris Chelios (112, 151, 140 PIM), Dirk Graham (139, 102 PIM), Denis Savard (110 PIM), Terry Ruskowski (120, 225, 252 PIM), Keith Magnuson (145 PIM), Pierre Pilote (162 PIM), Gus Mortson (147, 133 PIM), and Bill Gadsby (108 PIM).

7. Center Denis Savard posted the highest-scoring season as a Chicago captain when he tallied 23 goals and 59 assists for 82 points in 1988-89, his only season as skipper. Jonathan Toews registered 81 points in 2018-19, with 35 goals and 46 assists. Helge Bostrom registered the lowest-scoring season with one goal in 1932-33.

8. Chicago's first captain Dick Irvin became just as famous for his NHL coaching career as his playing career. Irvin was captain in all three of his NHL seasons in Chicago and posted 52 points in 94 regular-season games. The center retired in 1929 due to injuries and became a coach with Chicago, Toronto, and Montreal. He won four Stanley Cups and 691 career contests.

9. By the time center Doug Gilmour was named Chicago captain for 1999-2000, he was already a 17-year NHL veteran with several teams and captained of most of them. He was signed as a free agent in 1998 and took over the C a year later when Chris Chelios requested a trade. However, Gilmour suffered a season-ending injury late in 1999-2000 and was soon traded to Buffalo. He chipped in with 112 points in 135 regular-season outings with Chicago.

10. One of Chicago's longest-serving and most unsung captains was Dirk Graham. He was appointed in 1988-89 as co-captain with fellow forward Denis Savard and wore the C for the next seven seasons. The team never missed the postseason with Graham as captain, and he helped lead the club to the 1991-92 Stanley Cup Final. He also became the team's head coach for a portion of the 1998-99 campaign. Graham scored 343 points in 546 regular-season games with the Hawks.

CHAPTER 6:

STATISTICALLY SPEAKING

QUIZ TIME!

1. Who led the team in points in the 2007-08 season?

    a. Patrick Sharp

    b. Patrick Kane

    c. Jonathan Toews

    d. Robert Lang

2. What is the most power-play goals scored in a season by a Blackhawks player?

    a. 16

    b. 22

    c. 30

    d. 24

3. Goaltender Ed Belfour played 74 games in 1990-91.

    a. True

    b. False

4. Mike Peluso led the club in penalty minutes in 1991-92 with how many?

a. 352

b. 319

c. 408

d. 424

5. What is the most hat tricks scored in a season by one Hawks player?

   a. 6

   b. 5

   c. 8

   d. 4

6. How many goals did Chicago score in their inaugural season?

   a. 122

   b. 115

   c. 87

   d. 95

7. Which player had a 10-game goal-scoring streak in 1968-69?

   a. Stan Mikita

   b. Jim Pappin

   c. Bobby Hull

   d. Kenny Wharram

8. The highest plus/minus recorded in a Hawks season was +62.

   a. True

   b. False

9. How many points did the Hawks have entering the 2014-15 playoffs?

    a. 99

    b. 108

    c. 102

    d. 112

10. Duncan Keith had how many assists in 2013-14?

    a. 55

    b. 60

    c. 49

    d. 30

11. The most points earned by the team in a season is 135.

    a. True

    b. False

12. Which player led the club in goals in 1992-93?

    a. Brent Sutter

    b. Michel Goulet

    c. Steve Larmer

    d. Jeremy Roenick

13. Which player led the team in assists in 1972-73?

    a. Pit Martin

    b. Stan Mikita

    c. Dennis Hull

    d. Bill White

14. Phil Esposito scored nine game-winning goals in 1964-65.

    a. True
    b. False

15. Which goaltender had a save percentage of .883 in 1984-85?

    a. Darren Pang
    b. Warren Skorodenski
    c. Murray Bannerman
    d. Chris Clifford

16. In their 2009-10 playoff cup run, how many goals did the Blackhawks score?

    a. 57
    b. 80
    c. 61
    d. 78

17. Which defenseman led the club in shots on goal in 1973-74?

    a. Phil Russel
    b. Dick Redmond
    c. Doug Jarrett
    d. Keith Magnuson

18. Who had a plus/minus of +28 in 2001-02?

    a. Steve Sullivan
    b. Eric Daze
    c. Boris Mironov
    d. Michael Nylander

19. In the 1956-57 season, how many saves did goaltender Al Rollins make?

    a. 2,103
    b. 2,044
    c. 2,012
    d. 2,001

20. Dirk Graham scored 10 shorthanded goals in 1988-89.

    a. True
    b. False

QUIZ ANSWERS

1. B – Patrick Kane

2. D – 24

3. A – True

4. C – 408

5. D – 4

6. B – 115

7. C – Bobby Hull

8. B – False

9. C – 102

10. A – 55

11. B – False

12. D – Jeremy Roenick

13. A – Pit Martin

14. A – True

15. C – Murray Bannerman

16. D – 78

17. B – Dick Redmond

18. D – Michael Nylander

19. C – 2,012

20. A – True

DID YOU KNOW?

1. Since entering the NHL, to the conclusion of the 2019-20 regular season, the Chicago franchise has accumulated 6,556 points with a regular-season (wins-losses-ties-overtime losses) record of 2788-2736-814-166. Their playoff record stood at 264-270, and they had reached the postseason 62 times with six Stanley Cups to their name.

2. The franchise's best season points-wise came in 2009-10 with a record of 52-22-8 for 112. The worst season was 1927-28 when they went 7-34-3 for just 17 points. As for points percentage, the shortened 48-game, 2012-13 campaign saw Chicago earn .802 percent of points available at 36-7-5. The 1927-28 season was the worst at .193.

3. Individually, the club's leading goal scorer is Bobby Hull at 604, while Stan Mikita had the most points at 1,467, the most assists at 926, and the most regular-season games played at 1,396. Hull also scored the most goals in a season with 58 in 1968-69, and Denis Savard holds the record for 87 assists in a season in 1981-82 and 1987-88, as well as 131 points in a season in 1987-88.

4. On a per-game basis, Bobby Hull scored 0.58 goals per game to lead the franchise. Denis Savard had a team-best 0.82 assists per game and 1.24 points per game. In addition, Hull also leads the way in goals created per game, with 0.46.

5. There have been numerous physical players and enforcers in Chicago over the years, and this can be seen in the amount of time they spent in the penalty box. Defenseman and former captain Chris Chelios led the way with 1,495 minutes followed by Keith Magnuson (1,440), Al Secord (1,426), Dave Manson (1,322), and Phil Russell (1,288).

6. When it comes to goaltending, Tony Esposito leads in several categories. These include games played (873), wins (418), losses (302), ties/OT/shootout losses (148), goals against (2,529), shots against (26,905), saves (24,376), shutouts (74), and minutes played (51,734). Scott Darling holds the best career save percentage at 92.3, and Charlie Gardiner had the lowest goals-against average at 2.02.

7. Tony Esposito posted a team-record 15 shutouts in 1969-70, while Ed Belfour won a season-best 43 victories in 1990-91. Al Rollins lost 47 contests in 1953-54, and Esposito allowed the most goals against at 246 in 1980-81. Esposito also posted the best save percentage in a year at 93.4 in 1971-72, while Charlie Gardiner holds the best goal-against average in a campaign at 1.63.

8. If we check out special teams, we see Steve Larmer leads the club with 153 regular-season power-play goals while fellow forward Dirk Graham notched 26 shorthanded markers. Bobby Hull is number one in game-winning goals, with 98, and hat tricks, with 28. Meanwhile, Darryl Sutter has the team's best career shooting percentage at 19.5.

9. Mike Peluso holds the record for most penalty minutes in a season with 408 in 1991-92. Pierre Pilote had the best plus/minus in a campaign at +54 in 1966-67. Jeremy Roenick holds the record for 24 power-play goals in a season in 1993-94 and 13 game-winners in 1991-92. Dirk Graham scored 10 shorthanded goals in 1988-89. The best season shooting percentage was recorded by Ted Bulley at 25.7 in 1978-79.

10. In postseason play, Stan Mikita holds the record for 155 games played, 91 assists, and 150 points, while Bobby Hull has 62 goals. Al Secord served 266 penalty minutes, while Denis Savard notched 22 power-play goals, and Wayne Presley scored four shorthanded. Patrick Kane has 11 game-winning goals. Goaltender Tony Esposito played 99 career playoff games, with six shutouts, while Corey Crawford leads in wins with 48. Chuck Gardiner had a 1.43 goals-against average, and Corey Crawford's save percentage is 91.9 in 87 games.

CHAPTER 7:

THE TRADE MARKET

QUIZ TIME!

1. How many trades did the Blackhawks make in 2016-17?

    a. 10

    b. 9

    c. 6

    d. 14

2. In 2015-16, how many goals did the newly acquired Dale Weise score?

    a. 8

    b. 13

    c. 0

    d. 20

3. On October 18, 1926, the Blackhawks made their first trade in franchise history with the Toronto St. Patricks.

    a. True

    b. False

4. What did the club get in return for trading Andrew Ladd to the Atlanta Thrashers in 2010?

   a. A 2nd and 3rd round draft pick
   b. Ivan Vishnevskiy and a 2nd round pick
   c. Boris Valabik and Ivan Vishnevskiy
   d. Johnny Oduya and a 3rd round pick

5. Where did the Blackhawks deal Brandon Saad to in 2015?

   a. Dallas Stars
   b. Winnipeg Jets
   c. Columbus Blue Jackets
   d. New York Rangers

6. Who did the Blackhawks acquire in their first trade?

   a. Art Duncan
   b. Gord Fraser
   c. Art Gagne
   d. Babe Dye

7. How many games did Stephane Beauregard play for Chicago after being acquired in a trade for Dominik Hasek in 1992?

   a. 90
   b. 57
   c. 0
   d. 123

8. Chicago traded Johnny Wilson, Forbes Kennedy, Bill Preston, and Hank Bassen for Glenn Hall and Ted Lindsay in 1957.

a. True

b. False

9. How many points did Tony Amonte have in 1994-95 after being dealt by the New York Rangers?

   a. 41
   b. 35
   c. 39
   d. 28

10. Where did Chicago trade goaltender Ed Belfour to in 1996-97?

    a. Toronto Maple Leafs
    b. Nashville Predators
    c. Dallas Stars
    d. San Jose Sharks

11. Chicago traded Bryan McCabe to the Toronto Maple Leafs in exchange for Steve Sullivan in 1999.

    a. True
    b. False

12. How many trades did the club make in 1997-98?

    a. 8
    b. 12
    c. 10
    d. 14

13. What did Chicago trade to acquire Patrick Sharp and Eric Meloche?

a. Matt Ellison and a 2006 3rd round draft pick

b. Michael Leighton and a 2006 2nd round pick

c. Matt Ellison and cash

d. Anton Babchuk and future considerations

14. In 1991-92, the Blackhawks made seven trades with the Los Angeles Kings.

a. True

b. False

15. Who did Chicago NOT receive in a five-player trade with the Tampa Bay Lightning in 1994-95?

a. Jeff Buchanan

b. Tom Tilley

c. Alex Semak

d. Jim Cummins

16. How many players did Chicago trade to the Atlanta Thrashers in 2010?

a. 4

b. 6

c. 3

d. 1

17. Who did the club receive from the Buffalo Sabres in exchange for Henri Jokiharju in 2019-20?

a. Dominik Kahun

b. Ian McCoshen

c. Aleksi Saarela

d. Alexander Nylander

18. How many game-winning goals did Antoine Vermette score in the 2014-15 playoffs after being traded by the Arizona Coyotes?

    a. 4
    b. 3
    c. 2
    d. 1

19. Who did Chicago trade to the Boston Bruins in return for Al Secord?

    a. Ed Olczyk
    b. Mike O'Connell
    c. Tim Trimper
    d. Doug Lecuyer

20. In 2004, the club traded Alexander Karpovtsev in exchange for a 5th round draft pick used on Niklas Hjalmarsson.

    a. True
    b. False

QUIZ ANSWERS

1. B – 9

2. C – 0

3. A – True

4. B – Ivan Vishnevskiy and a 2nd round pick

5. C – Columbus Blue Jackets

6. D – Babe Dye

7. C – 0

8. A – True

9. B – 35

10. D – San Jose Sharks

11. B – False

12. C – 10

13. A – Matt Ellison and a 2006 3rd round pick

14. B – False

15. C – Alex Semak

16. A – 4

17. D – Alexander Nylander

18. B – 3

19. B – Mike O'Connell

20. A – True

DID YOU KNOW?

1. Chicago acquired center Antoine Vermette in February 2015 for a 1st round draft pick and Klas Dahlbeck from Arizona. Vermette helped the team capture the Stanley Cup that season by winning 58% of his faceoffs in the postseason. He also chipped in with three huge game-winning goals in the playoffs. Vermette then re-signed with Arizona as a free agent just a few weeks after winning the Cup.

2. The Blackhawks traded Alexander Karpovtsev to the New York Islanders in March 2004 for a 4th round draft pick and used it to take fellow blueliner Niklas Hjalmarsson in 2005. Hjalmarsson blocked 1,186 shots in his 10 years as a Hawk and posted a +109 rating while helping the club win three Stanley Cups.

3. When Al Secord was traded to Toronto in 1987, he was accompanied by fellow forward Ed Olczyk in return for Leafs captain Rick Vaive, winger Steve Thomas, and enforcer/defenseman Bob McGill. Secord was traded by the Leafs less than two years later, while Olczyk starred in Toronto. Vaive notched 94 points in 106 games with Chicago, while Thomas had 230 points in 334 games. McGill registered 36 points and 641 penalty minutes in 281 outings.

4. Chicago traded Steve Thomas and Adam Creighton to the New York Islanders in 1991 for fellow forwards Brad

Lauer and Brent Sutter and gave up offense for defense. Thomas had scored 80 goals and 164 points in 190 games in the previous three seasons. He then netted 258 points in 275 contests with the Islanders and 18 points in 22 playoff outings. Creighton played just 65 games on the island with 24 points, while Sutter scored 219 points in 417 games, and Lauer notched one assist in 13 contests with Chicago.

5. Ab McDonald was acquired with Cecil Hoekstra, Bob Courcy, and Reggie Fleming from Montreal in 1960 for Terry Gray, Glen Skov, Bob Bailey, Lorne Ferguson, and the rights to Danny Lewicki. McDonald notched 180 points in 265 outings with Chicago, was a +70, and added 25 points in 33 postseason matches. He helped the team win the Stanley Cup in 1960-61 and scored the Cup-winner against Detroit. The five players Chicago traded played a combined seven games for Montreal.

6. In March 1994, the Blackhawks traded Brian Noonan and Stephane Matteau to the New York Rangers for winger Tony Amonte. Noonan and Matteau were productive depth players, but Amonte would score 268 goals and 541 points in 627 regular-season games with Chicago and become team captain. He led the team in goals and points in three straight seasons, never missed a game in five consecutive campaigns, and missed just two contests in seven seasons.

7. The acquisition of defender Chris Chelios from Montreal in 1990 with a 2nd round draft choice for fellow Hall-of-Famer Denis Savard was a fine move. Chelios posted 487

points in 664 games and was a +120 with 48 points and a +26 in 65 playoff games. The Hawks then traded him to Detroit in March 1999 for Anders Eriksson and two 1st round draft choices. Eriksson was just a depth player, and Chicago drafted Steve McCarthy and Adam Munro with the picks. Chelios played 10 more years with Detroit and won two Stanley Cups there.

8. Jeremy Roenick was an elite center, but Chicago traded him in 1996. He was a restricted free agent seeking a five-year, $20 million contract. The Hawks didn't want to pay him and shipped him to Phoenix for Craig Mills, Alexei Zhamnov, and a 1st round pick. Chicago eventually signed Zhamnov to a five-year deal for $15 million. This meant they saved just $1 million a year while losing fan favorite Roenick, who had scored 596 points in 524 games and 77 points in 82 playoff contests. Zhamnov netted 424 points in 528 regular-season games with Chicago. Mills played 31 career NHL games, and Ty Jones, who the Hawks used the draft pick on, played just 14 NHL games.

9. Chicago center Phil Esposito had tallied 174 points in 235 regular-season games but wasn't a favorite of team ownership. Just before the 1967 NHL Expansion Draft, the Hawks shipped Esposito, Fred Stanfield, and Ken Hodge to Boston for Pit Martin, Jack Norris, and Gilles Marotte. Esposito would be inducted into the Hall of Fame, win five Art Ross Trophies, earn eight All-Star Team nods, and help Boston win two Stanley Cups. In addition, Hodge enjoyed two 100-point seasons after the deal.

10. Perhaps the worst trade in franchise history saw Dominik Hasek go to Buffalo in 1992 for fellow goalie Stephane Beauregard and a 4th round draft pick. Beauregard was then sent to Winnipeg for center Christian Ruuttu just 72 hours later. Hasek was named to the NHL All-Rookie Team for 1991-92 and appeared to have a great future. Ruuttu posted 90 points in 158 regular-season games in Chicago, while Hasek won two Hart Trophies, six Vezina Trophies, two Stanley Cups, and more before being inducted into the Hall of Fame.

CHAPTER 8:

DRAFT DAY

QUIZ TIME!

1. What year did the Blackhawks draft Denis Savard?

    a. 1980

    b. 1979

    c. 1981

    d. 1978

2. As of 2019, how many defensemen has the club drafted?

    a. 125

    b. 97

    c. 172

    d. 168

3. Chicago has selected six players 3rd overall in the draft as of 2019.

    a. True

    b. False

4. How many points did Kirby Dach score in his first 64 games with the team?

   a. 15

   b. 18

   c. 23

   d. 27

5. In the 2004 Draft, Chicago selected how many players total?

   a. 20

   b. 17

   c. 10

   d. 18

6. Which round was Brent Seabrook drafted in?

   a. 4th

   b. 2nd

   c. 3rd

   d. 1st

7. Who was the first-ever player selected by the franchise?

   a. Wayne Davidson

   b. Art Hampson

   c. Moe L'Abbe

   d. Terry Caffery

8. The Blackhawks have drafted 65 goalies as of 2019.

   a. True

   b. False

9. How many goaltenders has the team drafted through the 2019 season?

    a. 21
    b. 34
    c. 40
    d. 47

10. Who did Chicago select 20th overall in 2014?

    a. John Hayden
    b. Carl Dahlstrom
    c. Ryan Hartman
    d. Nick Schmaltz

11. Patrick Kane was drafted 1st overall in 2007.

    a. True
    b. False

12. Jeremy Roenick was selected where in the 1st round of the 1988 Draft?

    a. 5th
    b. 3rd
    c. 8th
    d. 7th

13. How many players did the team draft from 1967 through 1968?

    a. 1
    b. 2
    c. 4
    d. 5

14. As of 2019, the Blackhawks have drafted 124 centers.

    a. True
    b. False

15. Who was the first goaltender drafted in franchise history?

    a. John Peterson
    b. Eddie Mio
    c. Gilles Meloche
    d. Mike Veisor

16. What year was Ed Olczyk drafted in?

    a. 1984
    b. 1982
    c. 1985
    d. 1983

17. In 1978, Chicago selected Darryl Sutter in which round?

    a. 4th
    b. 9th
    c. 10th
    d. 11th

18. The seven players selected by Chicago in 1996 played how many combined NHL regular-season games?

    a. 3
    b. 20
    c. 257
    d. 44

19. The Blackhawks selected which player 214th overall in 2004?

a. Dustin Byfuglien

b. Bryan Bickell

c. Jake Dowell

d. Troy Brouwer

20. Chicago's first 14 players ever drafted played 19 NHL games combined.

    a. True

    b. False

QUIZ ANSWERS

1. A – 1980

2. D – 168

3. A – True

4. C – 23

5. B – 17

6. D – 1st

7. B – Art Hampson

8. B – False

9. C – 40

10. D – Nick Schmaltz

11. A – True

12. C – 8th

13. B – 2

14. A – True

15. C – Gilles Meloche

16. A – 1984

17. D – 11th

18. B – 20

19. D – Troy Brouwer

20. A – True

DID YOU KNOW?

1. After the 2019 Draft was completed, the Blackhawks had chosen a total of 518 players in the NHL Entry Draft in club history. They have also taken five players in the various Supplemental Drafts for American college players over the years. The Entry Draft began in 1963 with Art Hampson being the first-ever player taken by Chicago. However, he never played an NHL game.

2. Chicago didn't have much luck with their 1st round draft picks in the early years. Art Hampson was taken in 1963, Richie Bayes in 1964, and Andy Culligan in 1965, with all three of them never playing in the NHL. Terry Caffery was selected in 1966 and played 14 NHL contests, while Bob Tombari was chosen in 1967 and never played in the league either.

3. The first Chicago 1st round draft choice to play regularly in the NHL was forward John Marks, who was selected 9th overall in 1968. He made his NHL debut in 1972-73 and played his entire 10-year big league career with the Hawks. He racked up 112 goals and 275 points in 657 games, with 14 points in 57 playoff outings.

4. Even though they've been in the NHL since 1926-27, Chicago has drafted 1st overall just once. They took Patrick Kane with the pick in 2007 and hit the jackpot with him. As of 2019-20, the winger had won three Stanley Cups, a

Conn Smythe Trophy, a Hart Memorial Trophy, and an Art Ross Trophy. He was the first American-born player to win both the Art Ross and Hart awards and the youngest American to score 1,000 regular-season points.

5. The most successful draft pick in Hawks history, pointwise, was Denis Savard. The Hall of Fame center and one-time captain and coach ended his NHL career with 473 goals and 865 assists for 1,338 points in 1,196 games, with 109 points in 169 postseason outings. He holds several club records and milestones and played 13 seasons in Chicago in two stints.

6. The lowest-drafted Hawks pick to star in the NHL was forward/defenseman Dustin Byfuglien, who was taken 245th overall in 2003. He helped the team win the Stanley Cup in 2009-10 with 11 goals and 16 points in the playoffs and tallied three game-winners. Byfuglien played in five different seasons in Chicago before being traded. He was named a Second Team All-Star with the Hawks in 2007 and had 525 points in 869 NHL games at the end of 2019-20, with 50 points in 66 playoff games.

7. The highest-drafted goalie in team annals was Jimmy Waite who went 8th overall in 1987. Waite was the goaltending coach with Chicago as of 2019-20, but his NHL playing career lasted just 106 games. He played 58 of those with Chicago before being traded to San Jose in 1993. Waite then spent several years playing in Europe.

8. The lowest-drafted goalie in Blackhawks history to make a

name for himself was Dominik Hasek. The Hall-of-Famer was taken 199th overall in 1983 and went on to win two Stanley Cups and numerous individual awards and trophies with different teams. Hasek played just 25 games with Chicago before being traded in the summer of 1992.

9. One of the biggest busts in Chicago's 1st round draft history was Greg Vaydik. The center was taken 7th overall in 1975 and was also drafted 9th overall by the Phoenix Roadrunners of the World Hockey Association (WHA). Vaydik played just five NHL games with Chicago without scoring a point in 1976-77 and spent the rest of his career in the minors.

10. The only Chicago draft pick in 2019 to crack the team's roster in 2019-20 was center Kirby Dach after being taken 3rd overall from the Saskatoon Blades of the Western Hockey League (WHL). The 6 foot 4 inch Dach scored eight goals and 23 points in the 2019 regular season, with two game-winners, while playing an average of 14:16 minutes per game.

CHAPTER 9:

GOALTENDER TIDBITS

QUIZ TIME!

1. How many saves did Corey Crawford make in the 2014-15 playoffs?

   a. 598

   b. 569

   c. 473

   d. 544

2. Hugh Lehman recorded how many shutouts in the club's inaugural season?

   a. 6

   b. 3

   c. 5

   d. 10

3. Tony Esposito played 15 seasons in Chicago.

   a. True

   b. False

4. Who had 43 wins in 1990-91?

   a. Ed Belfour
   b. Jimmy Waite
   c. Ray LeBlanc
   d. Alain Chevrier

5. Corey Crawford won how many games in his first full season with the Hawks in 2014-15?

   a. 27
   b. 29
   c. 36
   d. 32

6. Glenn Hall posted a goals-against average of what in the 1960-61 playoffs?

   a. 1.96
   b. 1.78
   c. 2.02
   d. 2.10

7. Emergency backup goalie Scott Foster made how many saves on March 29, 2018?

   a. 14
   b. 7
   c. 10
   d. 8

8. Frank Brimsek played 4,210 minutes in between the pipes in 1949-50.

   a. True
   b. False

9. What is the most shutouts recorded in franchise history?

   a. 68

   b. 70

   c. 74

   d. 75

10. Murray Bannerman had how many assists as club goaltender?

   a. 10

   b. 9

   c. 13

   d. 7

11. Jimmy Waite played only 58 games in eight seasons with the team.

   a. True

   b. False

12. What is the lowest goals-against average recorded in a single season by a club goalie?

   a. 1.76

   b. 1.59

   c. 1.70

   d. 1.63

13. In 2001-02, Jocelyn Thibault won how many of his 67 games?

   a. 24

   b. 29

   c. 33

   d. 34

14. Carolina Hurricanes goaltender Cam Ward retired as a Blackhawk after his lone season with the club.

    a. True
    b. False

15. How many saves did Nikolai Khabibulin make in 2006-07?

    a. 1,491
    b. 1,723
    c. 1,600
    d. 1,505

16. Who had 20 penalty minutes in 1953-54?

    a. Jack Gelineau
    b. Ray Frederick
    c. Al Rollins
    d. Jean Marois

17. How many games did Cam Ward start for Chicago in 2018-19?

    a. 25
    b. 32
    c. 29
    d. 30

18. Who had a save percentage of .924 in 2016-17?

    a. Anton Forsberg
    b. Michael Leighton
    c. Scott Darling
    d. Corey Crawford

19. In 1971-72, what was Tony Esposito's save percentage?

    a. .899
    b. .927
    c. .930
    d. .934

20. Ed Belfour tallied 240 penalty minutes while in Chicago.

    a. True
    b. False

QUIZ ANSWERS

1. B – 569

2. C – 5

3. A – True

4. A – Ed Belfour

5. D – 32

6. C – 2.02

7. B – 7

8. B – False

9. C – 74

10. A – 10

11. A – True

12. D – 1.63

13. C – 33

14. B – False

15. D – 1,505

16. C – Al Rollins

17. C – 29

18. B – Scott Darling

19. D – .934

20. A – True

DID YOU KNOW?

1. A total of eight former goaltenders who played with the Chicago franchise are enshrined in the Hockey Hall of Fame. These are: Tony Esposito, Glenn Hall, Dominik Hasek, Ed Belfour, Harry Lumley, Charlie Gardiner, Frank Brimsek, and Hugh Lehman.

2. Goalie Hugh Lehman was nicknamed "Old Eagle Eyes" and joined the franchise in 1926. He was already 41 years old, and after playing the first full season, he became player/coach the next year and appeared in just four games. It's believed Lehman was the first netminder to pass the puck regularly to his teammates, and he scored a goal while playing in the Ontario Professional Hockey League (OPHL) between 1908 and 1911.

3. The Blackhawks have used five goalies in a season on several occasions but the most used in one campaign was six. This happened in 2003-04 when Michael Leighton, Craig Anderson, Jocelyn Thibault, Steve Passmore, Adam Munro, and Matt Underhill played at least once each. It was repeated in 2017-18 with Anton Forsberg, Corey Crawford, Jeff Glass, Jean-Francois Berube, Colin Delia, and Scott Foster.

4. When Scott Foster played in net against Winnipeg on March 30, 2018, he did so as an emergency replacement. The 36-year-old recreational goalie played the final 14

minutes after both Chicago goalies were injured. The full-time accountant saved all seven shots as the Hawks won 6-2. Colin Delia also debuted for the Hawks that night before leaving the game. This meant two goalies from the same club made their NHL debuts in the same contest.

5. Chicago got some outside help when they won the Stanley Cup against Toronto in 1938. Starting goalie Mike Karakas fractured a toe in the previous round, and their minor league goalie was in Winnipeg. Chicago wanted to use Dave Kerr of the New York Rangers, but Toronto said no. The Hawks tracked minor league goalie Alfie Moore down at a local bar that afternoon. He beat the Leafs 3-1 in the opening game that night after sobering up but wasn't allowed to play the rest of the series.

6. Samuel LoPresti of Chicago holds the NHL record for facing the most shots in a regular-season game at 83. He also holds the mark for the most saves as he stopped 80 of them in a 3-2 loss to Boston on March 4, 1941. He left the NHL during World War II to serve in the U.S. Navy and was inducted into the United States Hockey Hall of Fame in 1973. LoPresti's ship was torpedoed during the war, and he survived 42 days at sea in a lifeboat.

7. Gary "Suitcase" Smith holds the league record for the most losses in a regular season, with 48. He went 19-48-4 with California in 1970-71 with a goals-against average of 3.86 and an 88.4 save percentage. The Hawks acquired him in a trade in the offseason, and he turned things around by going 14-5-6 with a goals-against average of 2.42 and a 91.1

save percentage. He also shared the Vezina Trophy with Tony Esposito for the fewest goals against.

8. Tony Esposito was claimed in the NHL's Intra-League Draft in 1969 after playing 13 games with Montreal the season before. Technically still a rookie, he posted a 2.17 goals-against average in 1969-70 and set a modern-day NHL record by earning 15 shutouts. Esposito was named rookie of the year, won the Vezina Trophy, and made the league's First All-Star Team for his work.

9. Darren Pang is a well-known NHL television broadcaster who spent his playing days with Chicago. The undrafted Pang was the second-shortest goalie in NHL history at 5 feet 5 inches tall and was signed as a free agent in 1984. He made the All-Rookie Team in 1987-88, recorded a team-record six assists, and was a finalist for the Calder Trophy. However, his career ended during the team's preseason camp in 1990 when he suffered a knee injury.

10. Maurice "Moe" Roberts played just 10 NHL games in his extensive pro career but set two league records while doing so. In 1925, he became the youngest goalie in league history when he played for the Boston Bruins at the age of 19. In November of 1951, 26 years later, Roberts played for the Blackhawks when their starting goalie was injured during the contest. Roberts filled in for him even though he was the team's assistant trainer at the time. At 45 years of age, he then became the oldest goalie and player to play in the league. Roberts was both the youngest and oldest goalie in the NHL for over 20 years until his records were broken.

CHAPTER 10:

ODDS & ENDS

QUIZ TIME!

1. Which Hawks coach has 161 tied games on his record?

    a. Paul Thompson

    b. Bob Pulford

    c. Rudy Pilous

    d. Billy Reay

2. What is the name of the club's mascot?

    a. Screech

    b. Hawk Man

    c. Tommy Hawk

    d. Tommy Talons

3. Chicago became the first team to sound a horn when a player scored a goal.

    a. True

    b. False

4. How many years did Bob Elson serve as the club's play-by-play commentator on the radio?

   a. 20

   b. 15

   c. 8

   d. 10

5. Who did the Hawks beat in the 2014 Stadium Series 5-1?

   a. Pittsburgh Penguins

   b. Detroit Red Wings

   c. Washington Capitals

   d. Minnesota Wild

6. Which player took 414 shots, the most in one Hawks season?

   a. Jonathan Toews

   b. Patrick Kane

   c. Bobby Hull

   d. Stan Mikita

7. Who scored the franchise's first hat trick in 1927?

   a. Art Somers

   b. George Hay

   c. Babe Dye

   d. Gord Fraser

8. Chicago would go on a two-week road trip in November while the circus took over their rink, but have not done so since 2017.

   a. True

   b. False

9. In 2009-10, how many hits did the team dole out?

   a. 1,731
   b. 1,490
   c. 1,634
   d. 1,555

10. How many penalty minutes did Aaron Downey serve in 36 games in 2001-02?

   a. 64
   b. 52
   c. 76
   d. 48

11. The Blackhawks have won three of the four Winter Classic games they have played.

   a. True
   b. False

12. Which team did Chicago NOT face in the 2012-13 playoffs?

   a. Minnesota Wild
   b. Los Angeles Kings
   c. Detroit Red Wings
   d. Vancouver Canucks

13. In 2016-17, how many shootout goals did Artemi Panarin score for the club?

   a. 4
   b. 6
   c. 2
   d. 5

14. The Hawks scored on their very first penalty shot attempt.

   a. True
   b. False

15. How many goals did the Hawks score in 1989-90?

   a. 320
   b. 316
   c. 278
   d. 222

16. How many games did Billy Reay coach in Chicago?

   a. 867
   b. 659
   c. 1,012
   d. 978

17. How many shots did Chicago block in the 2015-16 season?

   a. 1,232
   b. 1,133
   c. 989
   d. 1,067

18. How quickly did Bill Mosienko score a hat trick on March 23, 1952?

   a. 25 seconds
   b. 34 seconds
   c. 60 seconds
   d. 21 seconds

19. Steve Larmer's iron man streak lasted how many games?

    a. 884

    b. 890

    c. 798

    d. 867

20. The team name was originally spelled "Black Hawks" until 1986.

    a. True

    b. False

QUIZ ANSWERS

1. D – Billy Reay

2. C – Tommy Hawk

3. A – True

4. B – 15

5. A – Pittsburgh Penguins

6. C – Bobby Hull

7. B – George Hay

8. A – True

9. D – 1,555

10. C – 76

11. B – False

12. D – Vancouver Canucks

13. A – 4

14. A – True

15. B – 316

16. C – 1,012

17. B – 1,133

18. D – 21 seconds

19. A – 884

20. A – True

DID YOU KNOW?

1. Hall of Fame goalie Glenn Hall played 906 regular-season games during his career until 1971, including an NHL-record 502 in a row for a goalie. He rarely wore a mask but faced his nervousness before each game by throwing up and then drinking a glass of orange juice. Darren Pang, who tended goal between 1986 and 1989 for the club, also shared the same vomiting habit as Hall.

2. When the World Hockey Association (WHA) started to compete against the NHL in 1972, the first NHL star to jump ship was Chicago's Bobby Hull. The Hall-of-Famer was offered a 10-year, $1.75 million contract by the Winnipeg Jets, with a $1 million signing bonus. He was twice named the WHA's league MVP and won three championships in the league. His 77 goals in the 1974-75 season was also a new record in the pro leagues.

3. The NHL created a new rule regarding the curvature of stick blades due to the Blackhawks' Stan Mikita and Bobby Hull. The line mates started experimenting by curving their blades in the 1960s, and the results became known as "banana blades." Goaltenders, who rarely wore masks in those days, were terrified since the curved blades meant the puck's trajectory was unpredictable. The league then created a new rule in 1970 which limited the curvature of a blade.

4. There have been 38 different head coaches in franchise history, with Pete Muldoon being the first in the inaugural 1926-27 season. The latest coach is Jeremy Colliton, who took over on November 6, 2018. Dick Irvin had three stints as head coach, while Bob Pulford had four.

5. The most successful coach in team history was Joel Quenneville who led the team to three Stanley Cups. Rudy Pilous, Bill Stewart, and Tommy Gorman each won one Cup. Pilous and Gorman were inducted into the Hockey Hall of Fame as builders along with fellow coach Tommy Ivan. Former coaches Dick Irvin, Sid Abel, Hugh Lehman, Ebbie Goodfellow, Charlie Conacher, and Denis Savard were enshrined as players.

6. The only Hawks head coach to win the Jack Adams Award as NHL coach of the year was Orval Tessier for the 1982-83 regular season. The longest-serving coach was Billy Reay, who spent 14 seasons with Chicago. He holds the club record for regular-season and postseason games coached and wins. Reay spent 1,012 contests behind the bench, with 516 wins, as well as 117 playoff encounters, with 57 victories.

7. A total of 23 head coaches were behind the team's bench for their entire NHL head coaching careers. The Hawks also had a pair of brothers coach the squad as Darryl Sutter held the job from 1992 to 1995, and Brian Sutter was head coach from 2001 to 2004.

8. The club has had nine general managers in its history. Frederic McLaughlin was the first in 1926 and was

followed by: Bill Tobin, Tommy Ivan, Bob Pulford, Mike Keenan, Pulford again, Bob Murray, Pulford again as interim GM, Mike Smith, Pulford yet again, Dale Tallon, and Stan Bowman, who has held the post since July 14, 2009. McLaughlin and Ivan are in the Hall of Fame as builders.

9. The Blackhawks finished last in the Central Division in 2006-07 and 12 points out of the final playoff spot. They owned the 4th worst record in the NHL that season but then won the NHL's Draft Lottery. This gave them the 1st overall pick in the 2007 NHL Entry Draft, and they chose winger Patrick Kane.

10. The team's fortunes changed in 2008-09 when they posted 104 points and made the playoffs for the first time since 2001-02. It was also the first time they had reached 100 points in 17 years. The Hawks made it to the Western Conference Semifinals for the first time since 1995-96 before losing the Western Conference Championship to Detroit in five games.

CHAPTER 11:

BLACKHAWKS ON THE BLUE LINE

Quiz Time!

1. Which rearguard scored 80 power-play goals for the club?

   a. Bob Murray

   b. Doug Wilson

   c. Brent Seabrook

   d. Chris Chelios

2. How many points did Duncan Keith tally in 2009-10?

   a. 63

   b. 74

   c. 70

   d. 69

3. Chris Chelios was assessed 1,495 penalty minutes, the most in franchise history.

   a. True

   b. False

4. Defenseman Pat Stapleton posted a plus/minus of what in the 1970-71 season?

   a. +43
   b. -11
   c. +48
   d. -58

5. How many points did Bobby Orr score as a member of the Blackhawks?

   a. 27
   b. 30
   c. 7
   d. 11

6. During the 2011-12 season, the Hawks' blueline scored how many points?

   a. 160
   b. 96
   c. 124
   d. 157

7. In his 10 years with the team, Niklas Hjalmarsson blocked how many shots?

   a. 1,201
   b. 1,186
   c. 1,157
   d. 1,053

8. Pierre Pilote played all 70 games in five straight seasons.

   a. True
   b. False

9. Dave Manson played 50 playoff games in Chicago and recorded how many penalty minutes?

    a. 176
    b. 114
    c. 203
    d. 245

10. Which defender scored 10 goals in 1994-95?

    a. Cam Russell
    b. Steve Smith
    c. Chris Chelios
    d. Gary Suter

11. Only two defensemen scored a point in the Hawks' first playoff run.

    a. True
    b. False

12. How many blueliners played at least five games in 2003-04?

    a. 11
    b. 15
    c. 8
    d. 12

13. Which defender scored 21 points in the 2014-15 playoffs?

    a. Brent Seabrook
    b. Duncan Keith
    c. Johnny Oduya
    d. Kyle Cumiskey

14. Dustin Byfuglien played 34 games in his rookie year with Chicago.

    a. True
    b. False

15. How many games did Paul Coffey play in Chicago?

    a. 18
    b. 31
    c. 10
    d. 27

16. In his rookie season, Keith Magnuson tallied how many points total?

    a. 15
    b. 33
    c. 27
    d. 24

17. How many hits did Brent Seabrook have in 2008-09?

    a. 224
    b. 230
    c. 202
    d. 165

18. In the 1996-97 season, how many blueliners played a minimum of 80 games?

    a. 4
    b. 1
    c. 3
    d. 6

19. How many penalty minutes did Steve Smith register in 1991-92?

   a. 316
   b. 304
   c. 289
   d. 310

20. In 1988-89, more Blackhawks defensemen had a negative plus/minus than a positive one.

   a. True
   b. False

QUIZ ANSWERS

1. B – Doug Wilson

2. D – 69

3. A – True

4. C – +48

5. A – 27

6. D – 157

7. B – 1,186

8. A – True

9. C – 203

10. D – Gary Suter

11. A – True

12. B – 15

13. B – Duncan Keith

14. B – False

15. C – 10

16. D – 24

17. A – 224

18. C – 3

19. B – 304

20. A – True

DID YOU KNOW?

1. There are 15 former Chicago blueliners in the Hockey Hall of Fame. These are: Al Arbour, Allan Stanley, Barney Stanley, Herb Gardiner, Lionel Conacher, Bobby Orr, John Stewart, Chris Chelios, Bill Gadsby, Paul Coffey, Pierre Pilote, Georges Boucher, Art Coulter, Phil Housley, and Earl Seibert. Arbour was enshrined as a builder, while the rest were inducted as players.

2. The longest-serving blueliner in Chicago history was Bob Murray who was drafted 52nd overall in 1974. He played 1,008 games with the Hawks and amassed 132 goals and 514 points, with 56 points in 112 playoff outings. Murray later served as general manager of the club from July 1997 to November 1999.

3. Although the Hawks once dressed Hall of Fame defenders and multiple James Norris Trophy winners Bobby Orr and Paul Coffey in their lineup, things didn't turn out too well for them. The two played just a combined 36 regular-season and playoff games with the squad and chipped in with six goals and 31 points, with Coffey earning just four assists in 10 outings.

4. The highest-scoring defenseman in Hawks history was Doug Wilson who was drafted 6th overall in 1977. Wilson scored 225 goals and 779 points in 938 games with 19 goals and 80 points in 95 postseason matches. Wilson won the

James Norris Trophy in 1981-82, and the three-time All-Star once led Chicago blueliners in scoring for 10 straight seasons.

5. Allan Stanley was another Hall of Fame defender who didn't spend much time in the Windy City. Stanley played the 1954-55 and 1955-56 campaigns with the club and skated in 11 games. He notched 14 goals and 43 points, but the team failed to make the playoffs both seasons.

6. Jack "Black Jack" Stewart came to Chicago in a nine-player trade in 1950, which was the largest in NHL history at the time. After arriving, the Hawks quickly named him team captain and an assistant coach. However, he suffered what doctors called a career-ending injury in December 1950. Stewart made a remarkable recovery though but suffered another serious injury the following season. The five-time All-Star walked away from the NHL in 1952.

7. Georges Boucher was one of four brothers who played in the NHL along with Billy, Bobby, and Frank. He played his final NHL season with Chicago in 1931-32. Overall, Boucher skated in the league from 1917 to 1932 and won four Stanley Cups. He would later become head coach of several NHL clubs. He passed away in 1960, just three weeks after being inducted into the Hall of Fame.

8. One of the biggest players of his era was defender Earl Seibert, who stood 6 feet 2 inches tall and weighed 200 lbs. The physical Seibert was Chicago captain from 1940 to 1942 and played 10 seasons with the club, winning the

Stanley Cup in 1938. He was a 10-time All-Star who was inducted into the Hall of Fame in 1963. This made Earl and Oliver Seibert the first father/son duo to be enshrined in the Hall.

9. One of the Blackhawks' most underrated and consistent rearguards was former captain Pat "Whitey" Stapleton from 1965 to 1973. Stapleton was claimed by Boston in the 1961 Intra-League Draft and re-claimed by Chicago in the same draft from Toronto four years later. The three-time All-Star scored an NHL-record 50 assists for a defenseman in 1969, but the record lasted just one year as Bobby Orr soon smashed it.

10. The Hawks had a great stay-at-home blueliner in Bill White from 1970 to 1976. He also chipped in with 30 goals and 179 points in 415 regular-season games with the club, with a +181 rating. The three-time All-Star retired in 1976 due to a neck injury and stepped in as interim Chicago head coach in 1976-77 to replace Billy Reay for the rest of the season.

CHAPTER 12:

CENTERS OF ATTENTION

Quiz Time!

1. How many assists did Alexei Zhamnov score in his first season with the Blackhawks?

    a. 31

    b. 37

    c. 42

    d. 44

2. Which center scored 13 game-winning goals in 1991-92?

    a. Jeremy Roenick

    b. Mike Hudson

    c. Brent Sutter

    d. Rob Brown

3. Stan Mikita scored a total of 550 goals as a Blackhawk.

    a. True

    b. False

4. Denis Savard earned how many assists in his career with the club?

   a. 886

   b. 758

   c. 813

   d. 719

5. How many goals did Jonathan Toews score in 2018-19?

   a. 35

   b. 41

   c. 29

   d. 30

6. Which center led the team in points with 36 in the franchise's inaugural season?

   a. Duke Dukowski

   b. Eddie Rodden

   c. Dick Irvin

   d. Mickey MacKay

7. In 2005-06, Jim Dowd was the oldest player on the team at what age?

   a. 32

   b. 37

   c. 40

   d. 38

8. Pit Martin scored three hat tricks in 1972-73.

   a. True

   b. False

9. Who scored 36 goals for the club in 2010-11?

    a. Michael Frolik
    b. Jake Dowell
    c. Patrick Sharp
    d. Jonathan Toews

10. Which center had a shooting percentage of 25 in 1985-86?

    a. Bill Gardner
    b. Denis Savard
    c. Troy Murray
    d. Rick Paterson

11. Dave Bolland scored 47 points in his rookie season with the Hawks.

    a. True
    b. False

12. How many game-winning goals did Troy Murray score in 1985-86?

    a. 10
    b. 9
    c. 8
    d. 7

13. Which young center had 97 hits in 54 games in 2018-19?

    a. Luke Johnson
    b. Dominik Kahun
    c. John Hayden
    d. David Kampf

14. Before arriving in Chicago, Michael Frolik recorded back-to-back 40-point seasons.

    a. True
    b. False

15. Blackhawks centers scored how many points combined in the 2012-13 playoffs?

    a. 52
    b. 39
    c. 65
    d. 71

16. How many faceoffs did Marcus Kruger win in 2013-14?

    a. 270
    b. 438
    c. 339
    d. 463

17. As a Blackhawk, how many hat tricks did Alexei Zhamnov score?

    a. 5
    b. 2
    c. 3
    d. 1

18. Which center notched more than 80 points with a +31 rating in 1972-73?

    a. Ralph Backstrom
    b. Pit Martin
    c. Lou Angotti
    d. Stan Mikita

19. Who scored 131 points in 1987-88?

    a. Mike Stapleton
    b. Brian Noonan
    c. Denis Savard
    d. Troy Murray

20. Jonathan Toews had a faceoff win percentage of 58.6 in the 2015-16 season.

    a. True
    b. False

QUIZ ANSWERS

1. C – 42

2. A – Jeremy Roenick

3. B – False

4. D – 719

5. A – 35

6. C – Dick Irvin

7. B – 37

8. A – True

9. C – Patrick Sharp

10. D – Rick Paterson

11. B – False

12. B – 9

13. C – John Hayden

14. A – True

15. D – 71

16. B – 438

17. D – 1

18. D – Stan Mikita

19. C – Denis Savard

20. A – True

DID YOU KNOW?

1. There are 12 former Chicago centers who are in the Hall of Fame. These are: Sid Abel, Billy Burch, Phil Esposito, Mickey MacKay, Dick Irvin, Stan Mikita, Denis Savard, Doug Gilmour, Duke Keats, Howie Morenz, Max Bentley, and Clint Smith.

2. One of Chicago's shrewdest moves was claiming diminutive center Steve Sullivan on waivers from Toronto in October 1999. He led the league with eight shorthanded goals in 2000-01 and would post 303 points in 370 regular-season games with the team. Sullivan was traded to Nashville in February 2005 for two 2nd round draft picks.

3. Unheralded center Eric Nesterenko played pro hockey from 1952 to 1974 and spent 16 consecutive seasons with the Blackhawks. He contributed 247 goals and 495 points in 1,013 games and won the Stanley Cup with the Hawks in 1960-61. Nesterenko led the league in shorthanded goals with six in 1965-66 and later acted in the movie *Youngblood* and was also its hockey consultant.

4. After being acquired in the infamous 1967 blockbuster trade with Boston, which saw Phil Esposito leave Chicago, Pit Martin carved out a fine career with the Hawks. The two-way center played 10 seasons with the club and won the Bill Masterton Trophy in 1969-70. He notched 627 points in 741 games in Chicago and added 51 points in 80 playoff contests.

5. Hall-of-Famer Max Bentley made history on New Year's Day in 1943 when he centered his brothers Doug and Reg. It was the first time three brothers had ever formed an NHL forward line. Max played in Chicago from 1940 to 1947 and won two Art Ross Trophies, a Lady Byng and a Hart Trophy with the club.

6. Clint Smith joined the Blackhawks in 1943-44 and proceeded to reel off three straight seasons with over 20 goals. He won his second career Lady Byng Trophy in 1943-44 and captained the team the following season. Smith set an NHL record at the time in his first season in Chicago with 49 assists in 40 games and then set another mark by scoring four goals in a period in March 1945. Smith played 202 regular-season games with the Hawks and notched 81 goals and 202 points.

7. Troy Murray was a reliable defensive center who won the Frank Selke Trophy in 1985-86 and was nominated for the award seven other times. He could also be relied on offensively as he chipped in with a career-high 45 goals and 99 points that season. Murray had two stints with the club from 1982 to 1993 with 488 regular-season points in 688 games and a +67 rating.

8. Between 1974 and 1978, Ivan Boldirev was a popular center with the Hawks. He missed just two games in four-and-a-half campaigns with the team and notched 335 points in 384 regular-season games. He led the squad in goals, assists, and points in both 1976-77 and 1977-78. He was also leading the team when he was traded to Atlanta

in an eight-player deal in March 1979. Boldirev went on to play 1,052 games in his 15-year NHL career.

9. Of the four Sutter brothers who played for Chicago only Brent played center. He was traded to the Hawks by the New York Islanders in October 1991 and spent the last six-and-a-half seasons of his 18-year career with the team. Brent racked up 217 points in 419 regular-season games and was a +46. While playing with Chicago, his brother Darryl was the team's head coach for two-and-a-half seasons.

10. When it comes to penalty shot success, center Jonathan Toews leads the way. The Blackhawks had been awarded 80 penalty shots by the end of the 2019-20 regular season. They had scored on just 18 of them for a success rate of only 22.5%. However, Toews had buried three of his four chances for a 75% success ratio.

CHAPTER 13:

THE WINGERS TAKE FLIGHT

Quiz Time!

1. How many points did Patrick Kane score in 2015-16?

   a. 88

   b. 105

   c. 75

   d. 106

2. Who scored 34 goals in his second season with the Hawks back in 2000-01?

   a. Bob Probert

   b. Eric Daze

   c. Chris Herperger

   d. Steve Sullivan

3. Bobby Hull went 13 back-to-back seasons in Chicago scoring at least 30 goals.

   a. True

   b. False

4. Which left winger had 142 penalty minutes in 2003-04?

    a. Tuomo Ruutu

    b. Travis Moen

    c. Kyle Calder

    d. Ryan VandenBussche

5. Patrick Kane won how many faceoffs out of the 51 he took in 2016-17?

    a. 12

    b. 50

    c. 7

    d. 44

6. Who scored 92 points in 1972-73?

    a. J.P. Bordeleau

    b. Dan Maloney

    c. Cliff Koroll

    d. Jim Pappin

7. This winger scored nine points in the Hawks' 1933-34 playoff run.

    a. Doc Romnes

    b. Johnny Gottselig

    c. Paul Thompson

    d. Mush March

8. Dennis Hull scored 302 goals, exactly half of what his brother Bobby scored while playing for Chicago.

    a. True

    b. False

9. Jamal Mayers led the club in penalty minutes in 2011-12 with how many?

   a. 91
   b. 123
   c. 87
   d. 56

10. How many power-play goals did Marian Hossa score in eight seasons in Chicago?

    a. 27
    b. 35
    c. 40
    d. 54

11. Steve Larmer never played less than 80 games in a season for Chicago.

    a. True
    b. False

12. Al Secord scored how many goals in the 1982-83 season?

    a. 47
    b. 33
    c. 54
    d. 60

13. What was Ted Bulley's shooting percentage in 1978-79?

    a. 28.2
    b. 22.9
    c. 23.4
    d. 25.7

14. A total of 14 wingers suited up for the club in 1979-80.

    a. True
    b. False

15. How many games did Wendel Clark play in Chicago?

    a. 5
    b. 13
    c. 27
    d. 30

16. In total, Michael Nylander recorded how many assists in four seasons with the Hawks?

    a. 117
    b. 78
    c. 114
    d. 136

17. Which winger had a plus/minus of +11 in the 2012-13 playoffs?

    a. Daniel Carcillo
    b. Marian Hossa
    c. Patrick Kane
    d. Bryan Bickell

18. Which season did Jim Pappin serve 94 penalty minutes?

    a. 1966-67
    b. 1974-75
    c. 1972-73
    d. 1965-66

19. Which winger averaged 0.83 goals a game in 1965-66?

    a. Fred Stanfield

    b. Ken Hodge

    c. Bobby Hull

    d. Doug Mohns

20. Steve Sullivan scored more power-play and shorthanded goals combined with Chicago than even-strength goals.

    a. True

    b. False

QUIZ ANSWERS

1. D – 106

2. D – Steve Sullivan

3. A – True

4. B – Travis Moen

5. C – 7

6. D – Jim Pappin

7. A – Doc Romnes

8. B – False

9. A – 91

10. C – 40

11. B – False

12. C – 54

13. D – 25.7

14. A – True

15. B – 13

16. A – 117

17. D – Bryan Bickell

18. B – 1974-75

19. C – Bobby Hull

20. B – False

DID YOU KNOW?

1. The former Blackhawks wingers who made it into the Hockey Hall of Fame in Toronto, Canada, are the following: Bobby Hull, Ted Lindsay, Bert Olmstead, Roy Conacher, George Hay, Doug Bentley, Harry Watson, Babe Dye, Michel Goulet, and Bill Mosienko.

2. One of the most famous hat tricks in NHL history came from the stick of Bill Mosienko as he scored it in a league-record 21 seconds. He notched the three goals in the third period against the New York Rangers on March 23, 1952, in the final game of the regular season. He then hit the post 45 seconds later. Mosienko played his entire NHL career with Chicago, was a two-time All-Star, and won the Lady Byng Trophy in 1944-45.

3. Bobby was definitely the star of the Hull family, but the input of his brother Dennis should also be recognized. Dennis played with the team from 1964 to 1977 and produced 298 goals and 640 points in 904 outings, with 67 points in 97 playoff encounters. He finished in the league's top 10 in goals for a season, shots, game-winning goals, shorthanded goals, even-strength goals, shooting percentage, and goals per game at least once in his career.

4. Steve Larmer is the franchise leader in power-play goals, with 153, and he notched 923 points in 891 regular-season games with the team. He won the Calder Trophy in 1982-

83 as the top rookie and holds the club's consecutive games-played streak at 884, leading the league in games played for 11 straight seasons. His brother Jeff also played briefly for Chicago.

5. Grant Mulvey pulled his weight with the Blackhawks from 1974 to 1982 and played 574 of his 586 career NHL games with the team. He played a dozen games with New Jersey and then retired due to injuries. He scored his first NHL goal as an 18-year-old, and in 1982, he notched five goals and seven points in a game against St. Louis to set a club record for goals in a game. He tallied 281 regular-season points for Chicago.

6. Feisty winger Ted Lindsay played most of his Hall of Fame career with Detroit but also put some time in with Chicago. He arrived via a 1957 trade with goaltender Glenn Hall while Johnny Wilson, Forbes Kennedy, Hank Bassen, and Bill Preston went the other way. Lindsay played 206 regular-season games with the Hawks and contributed 44 goals and 123 points while serving 385 minutes in penalties.

7. When Chicago won the Stanley Cup for the first time in 49 years in 2009-10, it was a huge achievement for winger Marian Hossa. He had played in two previous Finals with Pittsburgh and Detroit and lost them both. He then signed a 12-year deal as a free agent with Chicago, and it was third time lucky when the Hawks hoisted the trophy. He scored 15 goals in 22 playoff games that year to greatly help the cause.

8. The NHL record for goals in a season in 1965-66 was an even 50, which had been reached twice by Rocket Richard and Bernie "Boom Boom" Geoffrion. However, on March 12, 1966, that all changed when Bobby Hull scored his 50th and 51st goals of the campaign to set a new league high. He then wrapped up the campaign with 54 goals.

9. Doug Bentley played 11 full seasons with the Blackhawks. He captained the team from 1942 to 1944 and again in 1949-50. Bentley became the first Hawks player to win the Art Ross Trophy when he notched 73 points in 50 games in 1942-43 and then posted 77 points the next season. He also led the league in goals both of those years. He thought about retiring when his fellow Hall of Fame brother Max was traded by the Hawks in 1947 but changed his mind. Bentley scored 531 points in 545 regular-season contests with Chicago and was a four-time All-Star.

10. When Alexander Nylander was acquired by Chicago in a trade with Buffalo in 2019, he became one of the rare father/son tandems with the team. Alexander's father Michael skated with the club from 1999 to 2002 and posted 63 goals and 117 points. Alexander registered 10 goals and 26 points in 65 games for the Hawks in 2019-20 in his rookie season. His brother William Nylander currently plays with the Toronto Maple Leafs.

CHAPTER 14:

THE HEATED RIVALRIES

Quiz Time!

1. Which team did Chicago engage in a brawl infamously referred to as the St. Patrick's Day Massacre?

    a. Los Angeles Kings

    b. Detroit Red Wings

    c. St. Louis Blues

    d. Boston Bruins

2. How many games did the Hawks tie against the Montreal Canadiens?

    a. 98

    b. 103

    c. 96

    d. 115

3. Chicago has lost every Winter Classic game they have played as of 2020.

    a. True

    b. False

4. Who did the Hawks form a rivalry with after three consecutive playoff matchups from 2009 to 2011?

   a. Vancouver Canucks
   b. Calgary Flames
   c. San Jose Sharks
   d. Minnesota Wild

5. In their first nine meetings with the Las Vegas Golden Knights, how many games have the Hawks won?

   a. 5
   b. 7
   c. 4
   d. 1

6. In 2009-10 regular season, how many teams did the club go undefeated against?

   a. 8
   b. 12
   c. 10
   d. 6

7. Which team beat Chicago 9-1 on October 21, 1986?

   a. Quebec Nordiques
   b. Toronto Maple Leafs
   c. Buffalo Sabres
   d. Edmonton Oilers

8. Chicago and Detroit have played against each other more than any other NHL teams in the regular season as of 2020.

   a. True
   b. False

9. Which team beat the 1990-91 division-winning Hawks in the playoffs?

   a. Vancouver Canucks
   b. Toronto Maple Leafs
   c. Minnesota North Stars
   d. St. Louis Blues

10. How many times have the Hawks and St. Louis Blues met in the playoffs as of 2019?

   a. 9
   b. 7
   c. 12
   d. 10

11. Chicago scored 16-plus goals against four different teams in 1933-34.

   a. True
   b. False

12. Which team did the Hawks NOT face in the 2014-15 playoffs?

   a. Tampa Bay Lightning
   b. Anaheim Ducks
   c. Nashville Predators
   d. Winnipeg Jets

13. How many recorded fights have the Hawks engaged the Toronto Maple Leafs in as of 2019?

   a. 216
   b. 234

c. 174

d. 307

14. The Montreal Canadiens have beaten the Blackhawks five times in the Stanley Cup Final.

   a. True

   b. False

15. Which team scored 47 goals against the club in the 1967-68 season?

   a. New York Rangers

   b. Boston Bruins

   c. Philadelphia Flyers

   d. Pittsburgh Penguins

16. What was the score in a blowout victory for the Hawks against the Hartford Whalers on November 17, 1984?

   a. 13-4

   b. 8-0

   c. 10-1

   d. 7-0

17. How many teams did Chicago score 10 or more goals against in the 2017-18 season?

   a. 7

   b. 3

   c. 6

   d. 2

18. How many goals did Chicago score against the Tampa Bay Lightning to win their sixth Stanley Cup?

a. 5

b. 11

c. 8

d. 13

19. Mike Peluso was suspended for how many games following the St. Patrick's Day Massacre brawl?

a. 10

b. 5

c. 15

d. 2

20. Chicago has defeated the Detroit Red Wings three times in the Stanley Cup Final.

a. True

b. False

QUIZ ANSWERS

1. C – St. Louis Blues

2. B – 103

3. A – True

4. A – Vancouver Canucks

5. D – 1

6. C – 10

7. D – Edmonton Oilers

8. A – True

9. C – Minnesota North Stars

10. C – 12

11. B – False

12. D – Winnipeg Jets

13. A – 216

14. A – True

15. B – Boston Bruins

16. D – 7-0

17. C – 6

18. D – 13

19. A – 10

20. B – False

DID YOU KNOW?

1. The Blackhawks have developed several intense rivalries over the years especially with the NHL's Original Six franchises. Their all-time playoff series records against the other Original Six squads as of 2019 were: Boston Bruins 2-5, Detroit Red Wings 9-7, Montreal Canadiens 5-12, New York Rangers 4-1, Toronto Maple Leafs 3-6.

2. Chicago has met Montreal the most in the playoffs but have a poor 5-12 record for a winning percentage of just 29.4. They have also fared badly against Montreal franchises in regular seasons with a 183-331-122 mark at the conclusion of the 2019-20 regular season. To make matters worse, the Blackhawks have dropped all five Stanley Cup Finals against their rivals with three of them going the distance.

3. At the end of 2019-20, the Blackhawks had been involved in 108 playoff series and owned an even record of 54-54 against 22 different clubs. They had winning records in series against 12 of those franchises, with losing records against eight of them, and even marks with two teams.

4. Chicago has had the most success against the Ottawa Senators in combined NHL games with a record of 25-10-2 and a 70.3 winning percentage. Although they've struggled against Montreal with a 37.2 winning percentage, the NHL's newest franchise the Las Vegas

Golden Knights have been a nightmare for the Hawks. The teams had met nine times by the end of 2019-20 with Chicago winning just once for an 11.1 winning percentage.

5. When it comes to goals for and against in regular and postseason games combined, Chicago has had the most success against Pittsburgh with an average of 3.6 goals scored per game. The teams they've found the hardest to score against are Montreal and Anaheim at 2.5 goals a contest. The Hawks have averaged 4.4 goals-against when meeting the Vegas Golden Knights for their worst average while their 2.5 goals-against with Florida is their lowest.

6. Chicago is less than 300 miles of highway driving away from Detroit, and their closeness has resulted in a fierce rivalry. In addition, the clubs made their NHL debuts in 1926-27. The squads have met a league-high 820 times by the end of the 2019-20 regular season, including playoff encounters. Chicago had the edge in playoff game wins at 43-38, while Detroit was 358-286-84-11 in the regular season.

7. St. Louis and Chicago are also just under 300 miles apart, and it's no secret the clubs aren't fond of each other. In fact, close to 300 fights have been recorded in meetings between the teams. Chicago has won eight of the 12 playoff series against the Blues with a regular-season mark of 151-121-35-11. The Hawks beat St. Louis in six games in the 2013-14 postseason, with four of the contests going to overtime. The Blues then beat Chicago in Game 7 two years later and won the Stanley Cup in 2018-19.

8. A rivalry with the Arizona Coyotes has developed since they've become frequent trade partners with Chicago recently. Many Hawks ended up in Arizona such as Nick Schmaltz, Niklas Hjalmarsson, Jordan Oesterle, Vinnie Hinostroza, and Antti Raanta while Coyotes Christian Dvorak and Christian Fischer hail from the Chicago area. In addition, Arizona skaters Connor Murphy and Dylan Strome ended up with the Blackhawks. The rivalry should grow in 2021-22 when Arizona joins the Central Division.

9. One of the most infamous Chicago vs. St. Louis meetings was known as the St. Patrick's Day Massacre in 1991. Six players from each team were ejected, and 278 minutes in penalties were handed out in the brawl-filled contest. In addition, after reviewing the tapes, Blues defender Scott Stevens was suspended for two games, while Chicago's Mike Peluso and the Blues' Kelly Chase were banned for 10 games, and each team was fined $10,000.

10. One of the newer Blackhawks rivalries is with the Minnesota Wild, and it developed in the first round of the 2012-13 postseason. The two teams found themselves in the same division that season after NHL realignment and were previous rivals when the Minnesota North Stars were in the league. Chicago has met the Wild three times in the playoffs, with the last two meetings coming in 2014 and 2015, and has won every series. The teams also met in the 2016 NHL Stadium Series with Minnesota winning 6-1 at home.

CHAPTER 15:

THE AWARDS SECTION

Quiz Time!

1. The Blackhawks had won a total of how many combined individual and team awards as of 2019?

    a. 88

    b. 73

    c. 80

    d. 91

2. When did the Hawks win their first President's Trophy?

    a. 1990-91

    b. 1992-93

    c. 2012-13

    d. 2014-15

3. Chuck Gardiner won the Vezina Trophy in 1931-32. This was the first trophy awarded to a member of the Blackhawks.

    a. True

    b. False

4. How many times did Ed Belfour win the William M. Jennings Trophy while playing in Chicago?

    a. 2
    b. 0
    c. 3
    d. 4

5. Which year was a member of the Hawks NOT selected to the All-Star Game?

    a. 1985
    b. 1970
    c. 2014
    d. 2004

6. Who won the ESPY award for best NHL player in 2015?

    a. Patrick Kane
    b. Jonathan Toews
    c. Patrick Sharp
    d. Corey Crawford

7. As of 2019, how many times has the club won the Clarence S. Campbell Bowl?

    a. 7
    b. 10
    c. 5
    d. 2

8. Stan Mikita won his first Art Ross Trophy when he was 22 years old.

    a. True
    b. False

9. What year did Bobby Hull win the Lady Byng and Hart Memorial Trophies?

   a. 1961-62
   b. 1962-63
   c. 1964-65
   d. 1965-66

10. Which broadcaster received the Foster Hewitt Memorial Award in 1986?

   a. Bob Elson
   b. Pat Foley
   c. John Wiedeman
   d. Lloyd Pettit

11. Pierre Pilote won the James Norris Memorial Trophy three years in a row.

   a. True
   b. False

12. How many Blackhawks attended the 1961 All-Star Game?

   a. 3
   b. 19
   c. 7
   d. 10

13. Who did Glenn Hall share the Vezina Trophy with in 1966-67?

   a. Dave Dryden
   b. Denis DeJordy
   c. Jack Norris
   d. Tony Esposito

14. Joel Quenneville never won the Jack Adams Award as head coach of the Hawks.

    a. True
    b. False

15. Which player won the Conn Smythe Trophy in 2014-15?

    a. Patrick Kane
    b. Corey Crawford
    c. Duncan Keith
    d. Jonathan Toews

16. What was Corey Crawford's goals-against average when he won the William M. Jennings Trophy in 2014-15?

    a. 1.94
    b. 1.98
    c. 2.33
    d. 2.27

17. Who is the only coach as of 2019 to win the Jack Adams Award for the Hawks?

    a. Bob Pulford
    b. Mike Keenan
    c. Orval Tessier
    d. Billy Reay

18. What was Pierre Pilote's plus/minus when he won his first Norris Trophy?

    a. -10
    b. -4
    c. +54
    d. +31

19. Stan Mikita won how many Lady Byng Trophies during his career?

    a. 4
    b. 6
    c. 3
    d. 2

20. As of 2019, a Hawks defenseman has NOT been selected to an NHL All-Rookie Team.

    a. True
    b. False

QUIZ ANSWERS

1. D – 91

2. A – 1990-91

3. A – True

4. C – 3

5. D – 2004

6. B – Jonathan Toews

7. A – 7

8. B – False

9. C – 1964-65

10. D – Lloyd Pettit

11. A – True

12. B – 19

13. B – Denis DeJordy

14. A – True

15. C – Duncan Keith

16. D – 2.27

17. C – Orval Tessier

18. B – -4

19. D – 2

20. A – True

DID YOU KNOW?

1. The franchise has been awarded numerous team and individual honors in its history. These include: Stanley Cup (6), Clarence S. Campbell Bowl (7), Prince of Wales Trophy (2), President's Trophy (2), Art Ross Trophy (9), Bill Masterton Memorial Trophy (2), Calder Memorial Trophy (8), Conn Smythe Trophy (3), Frank J. Selke Trophy (3), Hart Memorial Trophy (7), Jack Adams Award (1), James Norris Memorial Trophy (8), Lady Byng Memorial Trophy (8) Ted Lindsay Award (1), Mark Messier Leadership Award (1), Vezina Trophy (10), William M. Jennings Trophy (5).

2. The Art Ross Trophy for the leading scorer in the NHL each season was captured by Roy Conacher in 1948-49 while Bobby Hull won it in 1959-60, 1961-62, and 1965-66. Stan Mikita holds the team record with four for 1963-64, 1964-65, 1966-67, and 1967-68. Patrick Kane was the last Hawk to win it in 2015-16.

3. Eight Chicago players have won the Calder Trophy as the NHL's top rookie. Cully Dahlstrom was the first in 1937-38 followed by Ed Litzenberger in 1954-55, Bill Hay in 1959-60, goaltender Tony Esposito for 1969-70, Steve Larmer in 1982-83, goalie Ed Belfour in 1990-91, Patrick Kane in 2007-08, and Artemi Panarin in 2015-16.

4. The Conn Smythe Trophy for the MVP of the playoffs has been won by a trio of Blackhawks. Jonathan Toews won it

for 2009-10, while fellow forward Patrick Kane followed suit in 2012-13, and blueliner Duncan Keith took it home in 2014-15.

5. Three Blackhawks have also had their names engraved on the Frank J. Selke Trophy as the league's best defensive forward. Troy Murray won it in 1985-86, while Dirk Graham was honored in 1990-91, and Jonathan Toews was the recipient in 2012-13.

6. The Hart Trophy for being the most valuable to his team during the regular season was taken home by Max Bentley for 1945-46, with goaltender Al Rollins following in 1953-54. The Hawks then won it four years in a row as Bobby Hull was honored in 1964-65 and 1965-66, and Stan Mikita won it the next two seasons. Patrick Kane then captured it for 2015-16.

7. Four Blackhawks have combined to win the James Norris Trophy eight times as the NHL's best defenseman. Pierre Pilote took the honors three years in a row from 1963 to 1965 with Doug Wilson winning it for 1981-82. Chris Chelios won it for 1992-93 and 1995-96, with Duncan Keith rounding out the list in 2009-10 and 2013-14.

8. Several Blackhawks have been rewarded for their sportsmanship, ability, and gentlemanly conduct with the Lady Byng Trophy. Elwin Romnes was the first in 1935-36 and was followed by three Hawks in succession. Max Bentley won it for 1942-43 and was immediately followed by Clint Smith and Bill Mosienko. Ken Wharram was

honored in 1963-64 and Bobby Hull the next season. Stan Mikita then won it twice in a row in 1967 and 1968.

9. From 1927 to 1981, the Vezina Trophy was for the team allowing the fewest regular-season goals. Chicago's winners were Chuck Gardiner (1931-32, 1933-34), Lorne Chabot (1934-35), Glenn Hall (1962-63), Glenn Hall and Dennis DeJordy (1966-67), Tony Esposito (1969-70, 1971-72, 1973-74). In 1982, the Vezina was then handed to the NHL's top goalie with the William M. Jennings Award for the fewest goals conceded. Ed Belfour won the Vezina for 1990-91 and 1992-93, with the Jennings being won by Belfour in 1990-91, 1992-93, and 1994-95. Corey Crawford and Ray Emery shared it in 2012-13, and Crawford won it again in 2014-15.

10. A total of 54 former Chicago players and officials have been inducted into the Hockey Hall of Fame. This includes 39 enshrined as players and 10 in the builders category. In addition, 11 members of the franchise have received the Lester Patrick Trophy. This award was created in 1966 and is presented by the NHL and USA Hockey to honor those who have greatly contributed to ice hockey in the USA.

CONCLUSION

You've just leafed through almost a century's worth of fascinating Chicago Blackhawks facts and trivia since making their NHL debut in 1926.

We surely hope you enjoyed refreshing your memory regarding your favorite NHL franchise and perhaps even picked up some new tidbits of information along the way. We've re-lived the team's highest and lowest moments in a fun, entertaining, and educational way.

Most die-hard Blackhawks fans could have probably written this book themselves based on their extreme knowledge of the club, but we've done it for you. We've gone over the history of the franchise's most storied players, coaches, general managers, and owners and listed the majority of their hockey accomplishments.

With the Blackhawks being in existence for so long, it's impossible to list every detail of the club in a trivia book. There are bound to be individual players and coaches that we missed, but you can perhaps add those when you feel the urge to challenge your fellow fans in a trivia quiz. In the meantime, we hope you arm yourself with this book while preparing for your next Blackhawks challenge.

The book is also ideal for trying to convert those who support rival NHL teams.

The Blackhawks have been involved in some of the NHL's greatest moments so far, and there are certainly more to come. However, these moments don't mean much if people like you, the team's loyal fans, aren't there to share them.

Thanks kindly for being a fan and reading the trivia book.

Made in the USA
Monee, IL
03 December 2021

83829240R00085